# Shelby Foote

## Twayne's United States Authors Series

Warren French, Editor
*Indiana University*

TUSAS 431

SHELBY FOOTE
*Photograph by*
*William Speer*

# Shelby Foote

By Helen White and
Redding S. Sugg, Jr.

*Twayne Publishers • Boston*

*Shelby Foote*

Helen White
Redding S. Sugg, Jr.

Copyright © 1982 by G.K. Hall & Company
All Rights Reserved
Published by Twayne Publishers
A Division of G. K. Hall & Company
70 Lincoln Street
Boston, Massachusetts 02111

Book Production by Marne B. Sultz

Book Design by Barbara Anderson

**Library of Congress Cataloging in
Publication Data**

White, Helen, 1914–
Shelby Foote

(Twayne's United States authors series ;
TUSAS 431)
Bibliography: p. 141
Includes index.
1. Foote, Shelby
—Criticism and interpretation.
I. Sugg, Redding S.  II. Title.  III. Series.
PS3511.0348Z94    813'.54    82-3071
ISBN 0-8057-7366-5            AACR2

# Contents

# About the Authors

Helen White is Professor Emeritus of English at Memphis State University, and Redding S. Sugg, Jr., formerly Professor of English there and at Georgia State University, is a free-lance writer. They are husband and wife and have published as co-authors several articles on Southern writers and, as co-editors, *From the Mountain* (Memphis: Memphis State University Press, 1972). Their joint articles have appeared in the *Delta Review, Mississippi Quarterly, Studies in Bibliography,* and the *Virginia Quarterly Review.*

Helen White is the author of several articles and editor of two bibliographical studies, *Anne Goodwin Winslow: An Annotated Check List of Her Published Works and of Her Papers (MVC Bulletin,* No. 2, Memphis, 1969) and *Jesse Hill Ford: An Annotated Check List of His Published Works and of His Papers (MVC Bulletin,* No. 7, Memphis, 1974).

Redding S. Sugg, Jr., has published articles on a variety of topics in about twenty periodicals ranging from the scholarly to the general, including *American Heritage, Atlanta, Smithsonian, South Atlantic Quarterly,* and the *Virginia Quarterly Review.* He has authorial or editorial credits for eight books, including *The Horn Island Logs of Walter Inglis Anderson* (Memphis: Memphis State University Press, 1973), *Mother-teacher: The Feminization of American Education* (Charlottesville: University Press of Virginia, 1978), and *Walter Anderson's Illustrations of Epic and Voyage* (Carbondale: Southern Illinois University Press, 1980).

# Preface

We think it remarkable that our little book should be the first general study of a body of work of such intellectual distinction and artistic integrity as Shelby Foote's. His books, whether novels or history, have been respectfully but superficially noticed in major review organs since he began publishing in the 1940s. Only since about 1970 have more detailed scholarly and critical treatments of his books appeared. The most important of these remains the special issue of the *Mississippi Quarterly* (Fall 1971) devoted to his work. The attention paid to Foote is still less than that accorded to other writers with whom he might be compared—in our opinion, usually to his advantage.

One explanation of this comparative neglect is that he began as a novelist and then devoted twenty years to history. Critics interested in his fiction experienced between 1954 and 1978 a break during which he published no novels. If, in the meanwhile, he published three large volumes of history qualifying as literature, the literary critics were slow to cross the genre frontier to discover the fact. Since Foote is not an academically qualified historian, professional historians for their part have been ambivalent toward his achievement in their field.

Foote's fiction has been more widely and seriously reviewed and received more scholarly analysis in France—where it has been just the interplay of his novels and history that drew interest—than in the United States. There was slight interest in a translation of *Love in a Dry Season* published in 1953, but since the mid-1970s translations of *Follow Me Down* and *Jordan County* as well as a new translation of *Love in a Dry Season,* with Maurice-Edgar Coindreau and Claude Richard among the translators, have appeared. These have been reviewed at length in the leading magazines and journals of Paris, ranging from the middlebrow to the literary and intellectual.

The most notable French scholarly essays on Foote to date appeared in the April 1977 issue of *Delta,* a journal only fortuitously bearing the name of the author's native region, published at Paul Valéry University in Montpellier. Devoted to *Jordan County,* this well-organized and focused issue amounts to a unified critical study. Its contributors, as the editor indicates in an Introduction, are intrigued with Foote's acting upon the belief that all history is narration and that the distinction between novel and history is obliterated in the art of writing.

Our purpose has been to give an account, largely descriptive, of all of Shelby Foote's work to date, from which it appears that it is after all very much of a piece. He has written in two kinds, but what he has written is unified in the sensibility of the author and his technique as a writer. One would expect that he would have been valued as a writer's writer, at least by literary critics, although one might be prepared to find that his literary qualities would meet with skepticism among historians. He presents himself as an artist in narrative, whether fictional or documented, and makes a claim for the validity of narrative in both kinds. In view of the intense concern with the structure of fiction among literary critics, on the one hand, and with epistemological problems among historians, on the other, both may find in the future more to interest them in Shelby Foote than they have till now.

Shelby Foote's work is to be understood against the background of his native place, Greenville, Mississippi, a little metropolis of the Yazoo-Mississippi Delta with a modest literary tradition. Discussion of it is not extraneous biographical material in a literary study but indispensable in appreciating his work, in history as well as fiction. Declaring himself first and last a novelist, he writes novels about the Delta. When he digressed to write history, the subject was the external event which most affected his Delta scene, the Civil War. He always meant to get back to fiction and has done so.

The Delta is a fact of geography and culture but also of literature. Discovery during adolescence of this latter aspect, chiefly in the works of William Alexander Percy of Greenville and William Faulkner, led Foote to his lifelong fascination with the material. We have sketched both aspects and Foote as an heir of both.

Between 1949 and 1954, Foote published five novels directly or indirectly concerned with his fictional property, Jordan County, and he returned to this material in his sixth novel, published in 1978. Our presentation of these books distinguishes, incidentally, their subject matter and style from those of William Faulkner. Jordan County is inevitably and properly to be compared with Yoknapatawpha County, and a further explanation of critical neglect of Foote may be the idea that his work is derivative in a questionable sense. He should be thought of, however, as a legitimate son of the master and credited as well with relationships to other branches of his artistic genealogy.

A special word is required on Foote's short novel, *Shiloh,* published in 1952, an elegant work in which experience of "the first modern battle," as Foote and others regard it, early in "the last romantic war," as Winston Churchill called the Civil War, is rendered through monologues by participants. One of these is a boy from Jordan County. *Shiloh* is a fastidious example of a type often abused, the historical novel. Since the battle is treated, of course, in *The Civil War,* two versions by Foote exist, one fictional, one not. We suggest close comparison. Our main insight is that, whereas in the novel the authorial voice is artistically excluded, in the history it is artistically deployed, with intriguing implications regarding issues in the philosophy of history.

For in the majestic *The Civil War,* art once again claims parity with science at a period when "scientific" history has been in question. The three volumes of this work contain approximately 1.6 million words, so perspicuously composed that the reader never feels *longueurs*—if, that is, he can read. We suspect that, all other considerations apart, the length of *The Civil War* has prevented acquaintance to say nothing of appreciation. But here, in one book, is material amounting to more than is usually found in a man's whole output during life. Yet it is one book, taking its place in the Foote canon, tightly organized, paced, and finished.

In dealing with a work of such dimensions, we have chosen to stress its qualities as literary art but not without attention to notions that history is science, not literature, or failing that, a research monograph and not a narrative. Foote leaves no choice. Narrative artist, he announced in a subtitle that *The Civil War* is, flat out, *A Narrative.* The indefinite article insists it is one account among others by an individual writer who does not deny or disguise personal tone and perspective. He pretends to no impersonal detachment, relies upon no graduate-school work force or professional support, claims no original discoveries or surprising revisions. Everything depends on the writing.

Unusual though such a presentation of a work of history may be, we have discussed *The Civil War* in terms of the writer's "vision," the narrative voice, the "plotting," and the "characterization." The facts are assumed to be correct on the basis of bibliographical notes Foote attached to each volume although he omitted footnotes in the interest of "narrative quality." Behind this application to history of terms normally used in discussing fiction is the belief that narrative *logic* is intellectually respectable. History consists, to some no doubt debatable degree, in the telling. But these considerations are not meant to obscure the finished artistic effect, and we have quoted Foote's text as generously as space has permitted in order to convey the texture of an admirable style.

When Foote consented to do a history of the Civil War, he was ready, he has said, to attempt "a new style of novel" which, in a sense, the history turned out to be. He was able to use in writing history everything he had learned, about organization and characterization above all, in writing his early novels. On returning to novel writing, he found that what he had learned about research in producing *The Civil War* now served him in fiction. His most recent novel, *September September,* is set in September 1957, and, though not primarily a re-creation of that short period, is suffused with what Foote could learn about it.

We feel and have tried to convey in the last short chapter a happy suspense with respect to Foote's work in progress, a major novel of Jordan county called "Two Gates to the City." He has had this novel in mind from the beginning of his career as a writer. From the first, he had a clear idea of his material and all that he intended to do with it—even the Civil War, at least with regard to the battles most directly affecting the Delta, was always part of it. He has been equally consistent in his idea of himself as primarily a novelist and would no doubt prefer to achieve a higher standard in the novel than in history. The achievement in history seems, nevertheless, to outweigh that in fiction. If, however, the novel in progress brings the Matter of Jordan County to a parity with *The Civil War,* Shelby Foote, already assured of distinction, will be recorded in history himself as a nonpareil of American letters.

Helen White
Redding S. Sugg, Jr.

*Fredericksburg, Texas*

# Acknowledgments

We are indebted to Shelby Foote for several helpful interviews, for supplying information on various points by correspondence and telephone, and for supplying the photograph of himself which is reproduced as the frontispiece of this volume.

The John Willard Brister Library at Memphis State University graciously allowed us the use of its copy of *Tournament* on loan both long-term and long-distance.

Selections from *Tournament*, by Shelby Foote, are reprinted by permission of the author.

All selections from the following works by Shelby Foote are reprinted by permission of Random House, Inc.: *Follow Me Down, Shiloh, Love in a Dry Season, Jordan County: A Landscape in Narrative, The Civil War: A Narrative* (3 vols.), and *September September*.

The selections from "Conrad Sits in Twilight" and "Antique Harvesters" from *Selected Poems*, by John Crowe Ransom, are reprinted by permission of Alfred A. Knopf.

We are grateful also to Staige D. Blackford, Editor, *The Virginia Quarterly Review*, for permission to use material from our article "Shelby Foote's *Iliad*," which appeared in the Spring 1979 issue.

# Chronology

1877    Advent of the author's grandfather Huger Lee Foote in the Delta.

c. 1908    Sale of Mt. Holly, Huger Foote's plantation, and removal of family to Greenville.

1915    Death of Huger Foote.

1916    Birth of Shelby Dade Foote (Jr.) to Shelby Dade and Lillian Rosenstock Foote in Greenville, November 17.

1917–1922    Family lives successively in Jackson, Vicksburg, Pensacola, and Mobile as the author's father rises in the hierarchy of Armour and Company.

1922    Death of father, Shelby Dade Foote.

1922–1925    Lillian Rosenstock Foote lives in Greenville, preparing to earn her living, and sends her son through the first three grades of school.

1925–1929    Lillian Rosenstock Foote lives in Pensacola as secretary with Armour and Company and sends her son through seventh grade.

1930    Return of Lillian Rosenstock Foote to Greenville as legal secretary and admission of her son to Greenville High School.

1931    Beginning of Shelby Foote's intimacy with Walker Percy, his two brothers, and their adoptive father, William Alexander Percy.

1934    Beginning of acquaintance with Hodding Carter, on whose *Delta Star,* later the *Delta Democrat–Times,* Shelby Foote worked intermittently from 1935–39.

1935    Beginning of acquaintance with David L. Cohn, editorship of high-school paper, the *Pica.*

1935–1937    Foote attends the University of North Carolina and contributes stories to *Carolina Magazine.*

1939–1940   Writes first version of novel later published as *Tournament*.

1940–1944   Military service beginning with enlistment in Mississippi National Guard leading eventually to commissioning and service as captain of artillery with Fifth Division in Northern Ireland; tried by court-martial for insubordination and dismissed.

1944   Marriage to Tess Lavery of Belfast, Ireland.

1944–1945   Several months employment with the Associated Press in New York.

1945   Service in United States Marine Corps.

1945–1947   Employment by radio station WJPR, Greenville.

1946   Publication of story "Flood Burial" in *Saturday Evening Post;* divorced from Tess Lavery Foote.

1947   After publication of story "Tell Them Good-by" in *Saturday Evening Post,* Foote decides to give up job to write full time; private publication of *The Merchant of Bristol* in Greenville.

1948   Completion of *Shiloh*; marriage to Marguerite Dessommes.

1949   *Tournament*; birth of daughter, Margaret Shelby Foote.

1950   *Follow Me Down.*

1951   *Love in a Dry Season.*

1952   *Shiloh.*

1953   Divorced from Marguerite Dessommes Foote.

1954   *Jordan County: A Landscape in Narrative*; removal to Memphis and beginning of work on a history of the Civil War.

1955–1957   Guggenheim fellow.

1956   Marriage to Gwyn Rainer.

1958   *Fort Sumter to Perryville* (Volume 1 of *The Civil War: A Narrative*).

1961     Birth of son, Huger Lee Foote II.

1963     *Fredericksburg to Meridian* (Volume 2 of *The Civil War*).

1963–1964     Ford Foundation fellow and playwright in residence with Arena Stage, Washington.

1974     *Red River to Appomattox* (Volume 3 of *The Civil War*).

1978     *September September*; judge of history entries, National Book Awards; Center for Southern Studies, University of South Carolina, sponsors symposium on *The Civil War*.

1981     Foote delivers Franklin Lecture, Auburn University.

## Chapter One
# Shelby Foote and the Delta

Shelby Foote has been committed since he commenced writing in the 1930s to the transmutation into fiction of his native place, Washington County, Mississippi, with its seat at Greenville, deep in the Yazoo-Mississippi River Delta. [Although a regionalist focused upon the particulars of a restricted scene, he has sought to endow his fictional Jordan County and town of Bristol with universality by giving them bearings on American history and the human condition in general and by artistic control of theme and point of view.]He professes the belief that narrative art is a means of arriving at truth in history as well as fiction, as near as it may be reached. Both kinds of writing are submitted to the discipline of facts, whether facts of individual experience and sensibility or documents of the past. Both the novelist and the historian must be ultimately the Writer, the term capitalized to connote seriousness about literary art and principle.

Although steadfast in his commitment to the creation of Jordan County, Foote has devoted more than half his life as an author to the production of a magnificent work of history, *The Civil War,* published in three volumes between 1958 and 1974. He signaled faithfulness to his vocation as literary artist by subtitling the result of his Gibbonian digression of twenty years into the historical kind *A Narrative.* The subject of his fiction has also been historical, dealing with events in his Delta scene at different dates extending as far back as the sixteenth century; the technique of his historiography derives from novel-writing. His work as a whole invites reconsideration of the provenance of theory of literature and literary criticism.

Jordan County remains the author's dominant concern, for the subject of the history that he chose to write is the grand external event influencing culture and personality in the Delta. He returned to fiction on Jordan County themes after completing *The Civil War.* It will be apparent, therefore, that, in considering Foote's work in both kinds, an

appreciation of the peculiarities of the Delta and of the author as a
Deltan must be central. It is significant, for example, that he only
accidentally became involved with treating the whole of the Civil War
in historiographical rather than fictional mode. Originally, he meant to
write novels about only the battles most directly affecting the Delta—
Shiloh, Brice's Crossroads, and Vicksburg. He actually produced only
the one on Shiloh, the success of which inspired a publisher to propose
to him a history of the entire war. An unmistakable fact about *The Civil
War* and, we believe, its fundamental excellence, is that the book must
be understood as good history specifically by a Deltan. It is a work of art
in which a particular author's sensibility, formed in the Delta—as any
author's must be formed by his given experience—has been candidly
deployed under artistic control.

## The Delta and Its Literary Tradition

The Delta is one of the physiographically, politically, and culturally
distinct sections of the state of Mississippi about the particulars of
which commentators on the Mississippi writers have sometimes demonstrated ignorance. Known to geographers as the Yazoo Basin, it
extends about two hundred miles along the Mississippi River from
Memphis to Vicksburg and about sixty miles at its widest between the
Mississippi on the west and the Yazoo and a range of bluffs on the east.
It constitutes the northwest quadrant of the state, containing 4 million
acres of deep alluvial soil. Once covered by a splendid hardwood forest,
it was rapaciously cleared after the expulsion of the Indians in the 1830s
and planted to cotton. The famous "flush times" of this part of the Old
Southwest resulted. These came late in the history of the slave-worked
plantation, produced a parvenu planter aristocracy, made Mississippi
one of the wealthiest states in the Union, and increased Southern
intransigency which helped bring on the Civil War. The Delta is
defined mainly by contrast with the hill country lying to the east and
north, the former characterized by the planter ethos and the latter by
that of the yeoman and subsistence farmer. "There are other areas of the
state which fostered the plantation economy, the Natchez region, for
example, or the Prairie country around Columbus," Elmo Howell, a
native Mississippian, has explained;"but the hills and the hill people
intrude into these areas so that the cultural lines are not so clearly
drawn."[1]

Howell observes, "No one approaches the Delta without a physical sensation, the sudden dip from the loess bluffs to the great alluvial flatness."[2] The major Mississippi writers have rendered the sense of entering the Delta as a world unto itself. For example, Eudora Welty—not herself of the Delta and only intermittently concerned with it in her fiction—thus introduces it at the beginning of her novel *Delta Wedding.* The point of view is that of a nine-year-old girl, Laura McRaven, who is traveling by the Yellow Dog (the local train which once served the Delta) to visit relatives who live on a plantation. She has started from Yazoo City at the southern end and been staring out of the window—"And then, as if a hand reached along the green ridge and all of a sudden pulled down with a sweep, like a scoop in the bin, the hill and every tree in the world and left cotton fields, the Delta began."[3] The time is 1923, the greenwood long gone so that

most of the world seemed sky. . . . The land was perfectly flat and level but it shimmered like the wing of a lighted dragonfly. . . . Sometimes in the cotton were trees with one, two, or three arms. . . . Sometimes like a fuzzy caterpillar . . . in the cotton was a winding line of thick green willows and cypresses, and when the train crossed this green, running on a loud iron bridge, down its center like a golden mark on the caterpillar's back would be a bayou. . . . In the Delta the sunsets were reddest light. The sun went down lopsided and wide as a rose on a stem in the west, and the west was a milk-white edge, like the foam of the sea. . . . Laura, looking out, leaning on her elbows with her head between her hands, felt what an arriver in a land feels—that slow hard pounding in the breast.[4]

Although William Faulkner, like Miss Welty, used Delta settings only occasionally, he probably contributed more than anyone else to creating consciousness of the Delta. As a native of the hill country, he had a perspective on it; Shelby Foote has frequently acknowledged his indebtedness to Faulkner's conception. He has said, for example, ". . . we in the Delta have been strongly influenced by Faulkner and so we were raised where we were and also reading Faulkner, which is a tremendously persuasive thing to encounter. It had an influence on us similar to the influence of the Delta itself."[5]

One of Faulkner's most influential renderings of the Delta occurs in "Delta Autumn," set in 1940, written from the point of view of a nearly eighty-year-old citizen of the hills, Isaac McCaslin. He has been going into the Delta for more than fifty years to hunt. He enters from the northern end by automobile, looking forward to the thrill of entry which in her way Eudora Welty's little girl also experiences. There is no mistaking the sensation—"the last hill, at the foot of which the rich unbroken alluvial flatness began as the sea began at the base of its cliffs, dissolving away beneath the unhurried November rain as the sea itself would dissolve away."[6]

For Ike McCaslin, the Delta contains the last vestige of "the big woods," scene of ritualistic hunting and rites of passage into manhood. During his lifetime, the woods have been steadily destroyed to make cotton fields and the planter way of life, so antagonistic to his own. Where once he drove thirty miles by wagon to camp, he must now travel two hundred miles by automobile to reach the ultimate remnant of the Delta where the Yazoo joins the Mississippi, "the territory in which game still existed."[7]

As he makes what may be his last trip to the Delta, McCaslin reflects upon its history, how "at first there had been only the old towns along the River and the old towns along the hills" and how from these points on its borders planters, first with slaves and later with hired hands, "had wrested from the impenetrable jungle of water-standing cane and cypress, gum and holly and oak and ash, cotton patches which as the years passed became fields and then plantations." Annually flooded, the land grew richer; today it "lay open from the cradling hills on the East to the rampart of levee on the West, standing horseman-tall with cotton . . . the rich black land, imponderable and vast, fecund up to the very doorsteps of the Negroes who worked it and of the white men who owned it; which exhausted the hunting life of a dog in one year, the working life of a mule in five and of a man in twenty. . . ."[8]

This is the place, the history, the people, the attitudes and sentiments—among many more, more particularly developed and sometimes corrected from the native's angle—to which Foote has devoted almost all of his fiction, while the Delta remained peripheral in Faulkner's. Foote has observed that "writers since Faulkner have tended to make Delta people sort of like hill people, under the Faulkner influence, but they are very different people."[9] Using a style, a narrative method, and often ideas very different from Faulkner's, Foote is nevertheless still working with what Faulkner has Ike McCaslin think of as "This Delta. *This land which man has deswamped and denuded and deriverred in two generations, . . . where cotton is planted and grows man-tall in the very cracks of the sidewalks, and usury and mortgage and bankruptcy and measureless wealth, Chinese and African and Aryan and Jew, all breed and spawn together until no man has time to say which one is which nor cares.  . . ."*[10]

The circumstances upon which McCaslin muses are those about which Foote writes in his own way. He might almost have been responding to McCaslin when he remarked in an interview, "Well, the first thing you have to understand about the Delta is that all this business about moonlight, magnolias, and Anglo-Saxon bloodlines has to go out the window.  . . . It is totally different from the hills, where the bloodlines are clean."[11] Ike concludes that the "ruined woods" do not "cry for retribution" for the very good reason that "the people who have destroyed it will accomplish its revenge."[12] Foote's fiction is an extended illustration of that revenge.

Since reviewers have been too ready to suggest that Foote's work derives in some discreditable sense from Faulkner's, it is important to understand how large an element in even so Faulknerian a passage as that just quoted is factual and thus as available to one writer on the Delta as another. Perhaps the point can be made by examining what Faulkner had to say about the Delta in a nonfiction piece. Much of what emerges in McCaslin's musing appears here as matter of fact. It was money-mindedness which sacrificed the big woods to a cash crop so that the Delta boomed, Faulkner says, "with simple money." He calls it "a troglodyte which had fathered twin troglodytes: solvency and bankruptcy, the three of them booming money into the land so fast that the problem was how to get rid of it.  . . ."[13] These troglodytes are prominent in Foote's family background as well as in his fiction. He is of the Delta as Faulkner was of the hills and has that deeper claim to the material.

In McCaslin's tone Faulkner conveys the hillman's mixed feelings of fascination and repulsion about the Delta and so contributes to an understanding of it by differentiation from the hills. "The Deltans," John N. Burruss has explained in the article on "Mississippi" in the *Encyclopaedia Britannica,* "pay homage to aristocratic plantation traditions." These are likely to include snobbishness with regard to the plain yeoman of the hills, who for his part stands rigidly on his dignity. Burruss adds, with a dryness more perceptible to Mississippians than to other users of the encyclopaedia, "The Hill people, however, do not defer to the Deltans, many of whose families originally came from the Hills."[14] The example of the Delta was a fatal temptation to some hillmen to grow cotton on land of a grade unsuited to row-cropping, which might turn a temporary profit but resulted in erosion and poverty in the long run.

John Faulkner developed the theme of the hillman tempted by the Delta in his novel *Dollar Cotton,* which should be considered in any account of the literary ambience of the Delta. The title refers to a fabulous price per pound that cotton once fetched and implies the differences in ethos between Delta planter and hill country subsistence farmer. The protagonist is a hill type—for some reason, John Faulkner placed his origin in the hills of Tennessee rather than Mississippi—who acquired land in the Delta. He played an epic part in clearing forest and cane brake, draining sloughs, and surviving the floods which enriched the land to produce magnificent cotton and make millions. But he could neither control a silly wife nor his feckless children and never understood his dependence on the market. The result is disaster as John Faulkner drives home the point that dollar cotton is a variety inimical to moral well-being.[15]

The literary treatment of the Delta which most directly affected Foote and against which his own work stands in contrast, often mordant, is William Alexander Percy's autobiographical *Lanterns on the Levee.* Foote lived during his adolescence and young adulthood in Greenville not far from Percy's house. As a schoolmate and friend of Percy's three young kinsmen and adoptive sons, especially Walker Percy, Foote was a familiar of the Percy house and heard *Lanterns on the Levee* discussed and passages from it read in the course of composition. Written from the center rather than from the perspectives of outsiders such as Faulkner and Welty, it is a belletristic performance in elegiac tones. All the claims Disraeli ever made for the landed aristocracy of Britain are advanced in behalf of the plantation aristocracy of the Delta. It was no doubt heady stuff for Shelby Foote, himself scion of a family of that class in reduced circumstances, a fatherless boy with literary ambition listening to the local man of letters his father's age.

Percy endowed the chief physical features of the Delta, which nobody can miss, with certain symbolic values which not everybody could feel unaided. He began with the Mississippi River, remarking, "Every few years it rises like a monster from its bed and pushes over its banks to vex and sweeten the land it has made," and devoted a memorable chapter to the flood of 1927, the trauma of Delta history which stands second only to the Civil War. Percy registered the effect of the Delta as a sea which other writers have also rendered, feeling it as a sea of deep soil rather than water, "built up slowly, century after century, by the sediment gathered by the river in its solemn task of cleansing the continent and deposited in annual layers of silt on what must once have been the vast depression between itself and the hills." His notion of the river as "the shifting unappeasable god of the country, feared and loved," which he expressed even as the United States Corps of Engineers was appeasing it, seems imbued with the fatalism, melancholy but proud, which he felt as heir of the unsalvageable planter tradition.[16]

Percy also dealt from his superior and sometimes precious point of view with the human geography of the Delta. Never questioning the virtue though recognizing the obsolescence of his own class, he was benevolently paternalistic toward blacks, scathingly contemptuous of poor whites—regarded as mostly interlopers from the hills—and condescendingly appreciative of other elements. These attitudes are candidly avowed, however, and tempered by self-deprecation so that they may be discounted and the lineaments of the scene clearly discerned. His personal position, moreover, was not without foundation. Regarded by some as racist and reactionary, he has recently been characterized as "a serious man" attempting to live by a failed tradition who embodied "greater authenticity" than the Agrarians.[17]

William Alexander Percy was born in 1885, the son of LeRoy Percy, whose plantation Trail Lake was twenty miles from Mt. Holly, the plantation belonging to Shelby Foote's grandfather, Huger Lee Foote. Huger Foote and LeRoy Percy occasionally had business as well as neighborly relations. Percy practiced law in Greenville and in 1910 was elected to the United States Senate over the populist James K. Vardaman in the last election of a senator by the state legislature. He lost to Vardaman at the next election, the first determined by direct popular vote. Seeing in his father's defeat "the rise of the masses," William Alexander Percy interpreted this as "evil triumphant, valor and goodness in the dust."[18]

If young Shelby Foote needed further illustration of the high romantic line on the Delta aristocracy, he had only to visit the Greenville cemetery where, after LeRoy Percy's death, William Alexander commissioned a memorial sculpture by Malvina Hoffman. It is the "figure of a brooding knight, sunshine flowing from his body as indicated in low relief on the stone stele behind, and the river at his feet." The statue is identified by "the one word, 'Patriot,'" and the richly sentimental effect is supplemented by Matthew Arnold's lyric "The Last Word" on the reverse of the stele.[19]

Foote was as much an heir to these social attitudes, thus monumentalized, as Percy—only he was a further generation down the line and several circumstances gave him perspective. He has always been primarily interested in the planter class and its progeny, but he has always wanted to know what was wrong with it, not just with modern descendants who do not measure up to traditional ideals or illusions but the grandest progenitors. Both of his grandfathers had been wealthy planters but died poor. His own father, deprived of land, had gone into business and died young. There were ambient memories of planter status, but he was born disinherited and demanded an accounting, as he grew up, from the preceding generations.

Another factor making for ironic detachment in Foote was the presence in his own background of one of what Percy called those "bright strands"[20] interwoven in the Delta population. Foote's maternal grandfather was a Viennese Jew who had immigrated to the Delta and established himself. He is one source of an outsider-theme in his grandson's fiction.

Finally, while Foote was under the influence of William Alexander Percy, he also came to know David L. Cohn and Hodding Carter, both protégés of Percy who wrote about the Delta, however, from a more modern point of view. Cohn's modernity was mostly a matter of popularizing the Percy version of the Delta in *God Shakes Creation,* later reprinted as the first part of an enlarged book, *Where I Was Born and Raised.* The Percy pastels turn into primary colors here. Elmo Howell has commented that "as a result of his friendship with Percy" Cohn "tended to idealize the role of the responsible planter" and adopted Percy's contempt for the poor whites from the hills.[21] He imagines the Delta as having passed through no raw egalitarian frontier times but as having supported from the first "a régime of the wealthy well-born planter . . . a society of gentlemen, overseers, and slaves." There was never a place for the poor white, who took to the hills, "raised large crops of children and meager crops of cotton. He worshiped a fierce God, hated aristocrats and Negroes, dwelt in poverty and darkness, and awaited the day when he might descend upon these fat [Delta] lands."[22]

If these assertions were not enough to deepen the skepticism of a young man of an ironic turn, Cohn's picture of the relationship between planter and slave in the antebellum golden age was guaranteed to do it. The whites who settled the Delta were, according to Cohn, "unique among pioneers" in that as offspring of planters in the older Southern states they possessed gentle culture and "the deep-rooted sense of responsibility common to their kind." Accustomed to wealth, "they were men of property moving with their families, their slaves and manifold possessions like princely patriarchs of the Old Testament." So long as the old order lasted, the Negroes lived an idyl in the Delta, simple happy creatures devoted to the masters who protected them. "The bonds of slavery were sundered. The stronger ties of affection held these alien peoples together."[23]

In Hodding Carter, Foote could see an instance of a more tough-minded, future-oriented approach to the Delta. Arriving in Greenville in 1935, Carter and his able wife, Betty, developed the *Delta Star* into the *Delta Democrat—Times,* an exemplary small daily; and Carter made a national reputation as a free-lance writer. He portrayed Percy as "born to the manor, a feudal, patrician manor," worthy heir of a Confederate colonel grandfather and Senatorial father.[24] Nevertheless, Elmo Howell speculates that if Percy had lived to witness Carter's success as a writer on the Delta "it is not likely that he would have rejoiced in his friend's acclaim." For "Carter was the extrovert reporter and later the entrepreneur of the Delta group [of writers], always in a bustle of organization and making speeches everywhere. In fact, though he paid high tribute to Percy . . . he looked upon him with a patronizing air as a representative of another age. . . ."[25]

The difference between Percy and Carter lay in their assessment of modernity and in their attitude toward writing. Percy remained the gentlemanly amateur while Carter became a pragmatic journalist and free-lance. To Percy modernity was dark although the darkness had its use as a motive for Housmanesque elegy; but to Carter, as one may read in his most widely noted book, *Southern Legacy,* modernity meant opportunity to liquidate the past, control the river, correct race relations, and balance agriculture with industry.[26]

For Shelby Foote, coming along as the third generation, Percy above all and then Cohn and Carter constituted a Delta literary tradition, brief but viable, and a context for literary ambition which few American towns the size of Greenville could offer. He shared with Percy preoccupation with the aristocratic past and could see Percy as an earnest of its reality or at least its unrealized potential. He, too, registered the dark of modernity. He tended to regard this, however, rather as the legacy of deficiencies in early plantation society than as the work of contemporary Yahoos, whose condition was after all part of the legacy. Neither was Foote so ready as Hodding Carter to take an optimistic, progressivist attitude toward the management of the Delta legacy.

## Shelby Foote and the Literary Potential of the Delta

Foote differed most fundamentally from the older Greenville writers in his attitude toward writing. Whereas Percy was a dilettante with a class interest to mourn, whereas Cohn was a middlebrow producer of a late species of local color, whereas Carter was a professional journalist and free-lance with an eye to the market, Foote, under the influence of early reading of Faulkner and Proust especially, declared a vocation as artist. In their different ways, the older men were important to him, not directly as models, but as instances of the possibility of a career as writer. Other Greenvillians, such as Ben Wasson, a writer and literary agent, also provided contact with professionalism and New York publishing. But Foote's approach to the Delta was conditioned by an ambition more serious than any of theirs: its potential as material for literary art was the main thing.

The Delta literary tradition centered in Greenville has continued. Although he has not lived there since 1954, Foote has maintained his connection as well as his commitment to the material. He has not entirely left since he lives in Memphis, traditionally the metropolis to which the Delta is oriented. In the meantime, Greenville has cherished its appellations as the Athens of the Delta or the Concord of the South. The Chamber of Commerce advertises culture as well as industrial incentive.

In 1968, a Memphis reporter announced that in Greenville "culture is a community product and writers lead the way in a city where 'art is living.'"[27] A local bookstore listed twenty-nine writers from Greenville, which thus outscored Faulkner's Oxford, credited with sixteen. Today the best-known writers from Greenville and its vicinity are Foote and his friend Walker Percy.

Long after he was himself established as a writer, Foote, speaking in Oxford, had occasion as a participant in a symposium sponsored by the University of Mississippi to express his views on William Faulkner's treatment of the planter aristocracy and brought in William Alexander Percy and the situation in the Delta. Dryly, a Deltan talking about a hillman, he stated, "Faulkner knew almost nothing about the planter aristocracy, or any other kind of aristocracy." More dryly still, a Deltan talking about himself, he added, "I come from a long line of planter aristocrats . . . and if that is aristocracy, we are bad off." The point he made about Faulkner was that in his fiction the treatment of aristocrats, particularly the Sartoris family, is inferior to the treatment of "the other side of Mississippi population, the other side being the other side from the Snopeses . . . people like Priests and Compsons, not aristocrats by claim or anything else." Foote's view was that "there simply aren't any aristocrats in Mississippi and probably never were any," and he thought "Faulkner realized that by the time he had written three novels."[28]

The matter is not quite so simple, at least in the Delta, as Foote's novels demonstrate. He can express such opinions partly in jest, partly because he does indeed come from a line—actually, from two lines—of planter aristocrats. The trouble is that the lines were disconcertingly short. The brevity of the plantation-based aristocratic condition, or claim and aspiration to it, the reasons for this and the effects on later generations and other classes of Delta folks are themes of Foote's fiction. Later in the symposium, Foote was brought back to his definition of an aristocrat. What he had to say illuminates his books:

I have said there are no aristocrats in Mississippi. I'm beginning to believe there aren't any aristocrats anywhere. I come from the Mississippi Delta where the credit is easy and the crashes are frequent. I don't personally know anybody who was around that part of the country, when I was born, that hadn't had a grandfather or great-grandfather who amounted to something considerable. Those down had been up, those up had been down. That's the way that country is over there. Now it is somewhat different out here if you have families lasting longer. But the first family around home, through what combination of luck I don't know, is the only one I know of that's held on to any of this world's substance over three generations. That just doesn't happen in my part of the country. Both of my grandfathers were worth close to a million dollars in the course of their lives; they barely had the money to dig the holes to put them in when they died. And that's standard over there in the Delta.[29]

He affirmed that William Alexander Percy was "the closest to an aristocrat that I've ever known, in these parts."[30] Percy had the background: the land and town house, the education—Sewanee and Harvard—and, what was remarkable, retained the substance: the tone and manners, and the literary dimension in addition. Lorn anomaly he might be, but he was almost enough in himself to prove the existence of an aristocratic tradition.

Even so, Foote made a distinction between Delta aristocrats and those of Virginia and South Carolina and a further distinction between Southern aristocrats in general and the British aristocrats he met during World War II. He said that aristocracy being by definition a product of ancient growth, "this whole business of Southern aristocracy is largely foolishness."[31] That foolishness, however, is a subject in Foote's fiction. The classes of Delta folks enumerated by William Alexander Percy are all present in Foote's work, but his emphasis falls on modern social and cultural amorphousness and alienation as the legacy of the aborted order. The Jordan County novels and stories turn on the question of why the munificently endowed landed families of the Delta were deficient in the business of "lasting longer."

In the last analysis, Shelby Foote seems to be persuaded that "the villain of the Delta, and maybe of the whole South, is the planter." The indictment, at least as delivered in interviews and symposia—the fiction is more complex—begins with the charge that the planter has conned other classes into following his lead by promising "someday you will be in my position and you will be allowed to do as I do." In former times, the planter pretended "to subscribe to the whole *noblesse oblige* notion" but nowadays says only, "I got mine." Not the least bitter charge is that the planter "has no respect for art in any form. He leaves that up to his women, and they have no respect for it either." The planter deserved to be "brought down by the Populist movement," as LeRoy Percy was at least in politics. Foote, the respectful and obliged friend of William Alexander Percy, came to see that Theodore Bilbo, cast as the devil in the Delta where Percy was "the man on the white horse," actually had the people's interest at heart "if for no other reason than to get their vote." But "LeRoy Percy, that honorable man, had his own concerns to look after."[32]

## The Foote Family

It will be apparent that Shelby Foote takes a clear-eyed perspective on his own antecedents very diferent from the sentimental and unsystematic—though often engagingly gossipy—genealogizing common among good Southern families. The Foote family arrived in Mississippi in the person of Shelby Foote's great-grandfather Hezekiah William Foote, who settled, not in the Delta, but in Noxubee County near Macon. This is located in the Black Prairie Region lying in the east central part of the state. It is drained by the Tombigbee River and was oriented, therefore, to Mobile. Hezekiah and his bride, born Mary Dade, were natives of Chester County, South Carolina, who migrated to Mississippi at an unknown date well before the Civil War. There were connections with Hugers and Lees, and Mary Dade Foote was a descendant of the Washingtons.

Hezekiah Foote studied law, became clerk of circuit court, and prospered as a planter. By 1861, he owned a hundred slaves and cultivated a thousand acres. He opposed secession but was loyal to the Confederacy once it was established and served in its army as an officer at Shiloh and other engagements. After service in the Confederate army, he was colonel of militia in the Prairie and in 1865 became judge of circuit court, located at Columbus, but retired in protest against Reconstruction policies. In 1875, he was prominent in the reaction which ended Reconstruction in Mississippi. At some period, he acquired additional land, a "prairie farm" of five hundred acres and, more notably, a stock farm of a thousand acres, which was an advanced enterprise for the times.

Mary Dade Foote died in 1855, having given birth that year to Shelby Foote's grandfather, Huger Lee Foote. Hezekiah married again three times, and apparently through one of his wives acquired Egremont, a plantation of three thousand acres on Deer Creek in Sharkey County, which adjoins Washington County in the Delta. He evidently enlarged Egremont by adding adjacent acreage and bought two other plantations, Mounds, also in Sharkey County, and Mt. Holly, on the shores of Lake Washington in Washington County.

To manage these properties, Hezekiah, who seems never to have gone to the Delta, installed his son Huger at Mounds in 1877, when Huger was twenty-two years of age. Huger Foote had been educated at Bryant and Stratton's Commercial College in Cincinnati and Eastman College in Poughkeepsie. He worked for two years as a merchant in Macon and then, till 1877, at Haney Grove, Texas. In the Delta, he is said to have produced six or seven hundred bales of cotton annually. In 1885, he was elected sheriff of Sharkey County and served as state senator from the 20th District in 1887 and 1889. Huger Foote married and lost his first wife in 1878 and in 1882 married Kate Shelby, the novelist's grandmother; his father, Shelby Dade Foote, was born at Mounds Plantation, near Rolling Fork. There a family cemetery was established, in which Shelby Foote expects eventually to lie.

But at some point Huger Foote moved his family to Mt. Holly, which he was in process of buying from his father, who forgave the balance due in his will. It is this place, with its Italianate villa in soft red brick, containing some thirty rooms, which is the model for the second mansion on Solitaire, the plantation which is at the center of Foote's fiction. Huger Foote sold Mt. Holly about 1908 and moved his family to Greenville, where he rented a big house on Broadway; by the time he died he had lost his fortune.[33]

Shelby Foote's maternal grandfather was Morris Rosenstock, to whom we have alluded. He was reticent about his origins in Austria but emigrated to the Delta in the 1880s. He became manager of the Peters plantation near Avon in Washington County and married Minnie Peters, the heiress. Through the production, ginning, and brokerage of cotton Morris Rosenstock became wealthy and also lived on Broadway in Greenville. In the market crash of 1921, the year his grandson turned five, Morris Rosenstock was ruined. He lived until 1927, long enough to win the affectionate remembrance of Shelby Foote.[34]

The details of Shelby Foote's family background which we have rehearsed are all directly relevant to his work and will be referred to from time to time in our discussion. They appear, mutatis mutandis, as elements in his fiction, exemplify what he sees as the classic predicament of the Delta aristocracy, and provide in a more general sense the grounding of his treatment of the Civil War. Huger Lee Foote is the personage who triggered his fictional inquiry into the past, personifying the main line in the development of the Delta planter society. Morris Rosenstock, the grandfather whom the novelist actually knew, is a source of personal particulars distributed among various characters in the books but, more importantly, a source of perspective. Foote has stressed as a difference between the Delta and the hills the presence of a more mixed and cosmopolitan population in the Delta, of which his Viennese grandfather was an instance. "I was perfectly aware that there was a world outside," Foote has said, "because my grandfather came from that world."[35]

In providing us information about his own life, Shelby Foote remarked that he could offer only the short and simple annals of a poor writer. It was a pleasant way of emphasizing his dedication since adolescence to writing, of implying a certain regret that he could only write about instead of live his heritage, and of hinting the proper use of details, genealogical and biographical, in discussing his books. He exemplifies his generation of American writers in his commitment to the quite serious idea of the writer as artist. None of his books is an advertisement of himself, and he has not exploited himself as a performing personality.

Born November 17, 1916, in Greenville, he lived until his sixth year in a series of towns—Jackson and Vicksburg, Pensacola, and Mobile—while his father pursued a career with Armour and Company. Shelby Dade Foote was rapidly promoted and finally moved to Mobile when he became the company's Southern regional superintendent. Shortly afterward, he became ill and unexpectedly died. His widow, Lillian Rosenstock Foote, and son returned to Greenville to live. The mother clerked in a gift shop while taking secretarial training and in 1925 moved with her son to Pensacola, where Armour and Company employed her. Shelby, having attended the first three grades of school in Greenville, completed the seventh in Pensacola before he and his mother went back to Greenville in 1929. She worked thereafter as a legal secretary, and he entered high school.

During his high-school years, Shelby Foote began to think of himself as a writer and—if the character Asa in his first novel, *Tournament,* may be read as autobiographical—knew from the start what he wanted to write about. Meeting the Percy boys and William Alexander Percy, he entered an ambience favorable to the development of his ambition. He recalls the impact, when he was sixteen, of reading William Faulkner's *Light in August.* It brought home the feasibility of rural and small-town Mississippi as material for literature and literature as a way of claiming the land he had not inherited. Greenville High School, like schools in many small and large Southern towns in those years, was academically oriented, and Foote had some effective teachers. He came to know Hodding Carter, David Cohn, and Ben Wasson, as we have indicated, and through them obtained bearings on writing as a career.

Following Walker Percy to the University of North Carolina in 1935, Foote stayed two years and did not take a degree. He remembers chiefly the pleasures of the stacks and reading rooms of Wilson Library, the first considerable collection to which he had had access. He contributed eight stories, some of which broach his Jordan County themes, to the undergraduate *Carolina Magazine*.[36] From wide independent reading, he chose Proust to associate with Faulkner as familiar spirits, Faulkner for reasons directly relevant to the Delta material as we have said, Proust and Faulkner, too, for their preoccupation with time and the perduration of the past.

After leaving Chapel Hill, Foote returned to Greenville and wrote the first version of *Tournament*. He tried to publish this but was told by the editor Harold Strauss of Alfred A. Knopf that it was too experimental and should be held for revision.[37] Feeling that he "should be in the war to stop Hitler" and—if we may again draw an inference from his fiction—that a Mississippi male was bound to seize every opportunity for military exploits, he joined the Mississippi National Guard in October 1939. His writing was interrupted when the guard was mobilized into federal service the next year.

Foote entered the service as an artillery sergeant, qualified for Officer Candidate School, and was commissioned in 1942. He was promoted to captain and eventually posted to Great Britain. While at a base in Northern Ireland, he crossed a superior who accused him of insubordination. The precipitating incident was Foote's being in Belfast without leave to see the Irish girl he was courting and whom he married. He was court-martialed and dismissed from the service in 1944. On returning to the United States, he worked briefly for the Associated Press in New York and felt for the first time in his life "truly disoriented."[38] But he spent his days off reading Proust and Browning, both of whom have had effect on his ideas and practice as a writer. In January 1945, he enlisted in the United States Marine Corps and served in the combat intelligence branch until the following November.

He returned to Greenville and resumed writing while holding various jobs as construction worker, radio copywriter, and reporter for the *Delta Democrat-Times*. In 1946, he was divorced from his Irish wife.

The primary literary project was the rewriting of *Tournament,* partly, he has said, to remove obvious influences of James Joyce and Thomas Wolfe.[39] The first item he sold was a story adapted from an episode in the novel which appeared under the title "Flood Burial" in the *Saturday Evening Post* for 7 September 1946. Another episode from the novel was separately published in 1947 as a slim book entitled *The Merchant of Bristol* and dedicated to Walker Percy. The publisher was the Levee Press, which Hodding Carter and others had established in Greenville. As an author published by this shortlived enterprise, Foote was in the company of William Faulkner, William Alexander Percy, and Eudora Welty. When *Tournament* was published in 1949 by the Dial Press, 750 copies were sold in Greenville, which in this further way proved supportive of local talent.

While reworking *Tournament,* Foote was also intent upon the impact in Mississippi and the Delta of what started out, at least in some romantic contemporary minds, as the great historical tournament, the Civil War. He conceived a treatment, in historical novels, of the battles which directly affected the state. He meant to write a trilogy about Shiloh, Brice's Crossroads, and Vicksburg but in the event produced only *Shiloh,* written in 1948 but not published until 1952. In the meantime, he had published the second and third novels about Jordan County, *Follow Me Down* (1950) and *Love in a Dry Season* (1951).

The Greenville period from 1946 to 1954 was extraordinarily productive and brought Foote recognition, although only *Shiloh* enjoyed a large distribution. This period culminated with the publication in 1954 of *Jordan County: A Landscape in Narrative,* comprising interrelated stories some of which were written as early as 1947.[40] Foote remarried in 1948, became the father of a daughter in 1949, and was divorced in 1953.

His removal to Memphis the next year began a new epoch in both his personal life and his work. He had made a series of approaches to the Matter of Jordan County and felt ready for a different kind of novel altogether—not a change of subject, but of technique. *Shiloh* represented a direction that might have been explored further. Random House, however, impressed with that novel, invited him to write a short history of the entire Civil War in anticipation of the centennial of the conflict. The work, originally contemplated as running about 250,000 words, took hold of Foote's imagination and led to intriguing technical considerations. The application of novelistic technique to historiography satisfied the instinct he had, after *Jordan County,* to change his methods. The short history grew to the three volumes and 1.6 million words of *The Civil War.* In 1956, Foote was married to Gwyn Rainer. A son, Huger Lee II, was born to them in 1961, and the family continues to live in Memphis.

Throughout the twenty years dominated by the production of *The Civil War,* Foote professed the intention to resume writing fiction about Jordan County. He affirmed this by reprinting in 1964 *Follow Me Down, Jordan County,* and *Love in a Dry Season* in the one-volume edition entitled *Three Novels.* The omission of *Tournament* was intentional, for he had come to regard it as a quarry for Jordan County themes and decided to remove it from the canon.

Following publication of the final volume of *The Civil War* in 1974, Foote made his turn back to Jordan County and published the novel *September September* in 1978. He spoke of this as an "action story" intended to get his hand as a novelist back in. Today he is at work on a major novel of Jordan County to be called "Two Gates to the City."

## Chapter Two

# The Jordan County Story Begins: *Tournament* and *Follow Me Down*

## The Matter of Jordan County

Between 1949 and 1954, Shelby Foote published three novels and a book of related shorter pieces which still comprise, pending completion and publication of "Two Gates to the City," the fictions set in Jordan County. These may be described as "takes" of Jordan County at different points in history, from encounters between whites and Indians at the end of the eighteenth century (with allusions to still earlier times) to about 1950. The books and stories are intelligible if read separately, but each gains color and substance if read in relation to all the others. They exhibit a kind of unity of place, i.e., place-through-time, as suggested by the subtitle *A Landscape in Narrative,* which Foote gave his fifth book, *Jordan County.* They are further unified by the quality of the author's vision and certain persistent interpretations, such as his analysis of the planter, and by the recurrence of characters or the introduction of their forebears and descendants.

Jordan County is a considered invitation to comparison with the work of William Faulkner. Foote meant the comparison to issue in distinction, and it does. The differences of culture and character between the cash-cropping Delta and the more straitened subsistence-farming hills gave the younger novelist room to develop his own field. Shelby Foote, born to the Delta, had from the first his own sense of territory, lived within it, and further distinguished his fictional property from Faulkner's by developing his own technique and style. The occasional Faulknerian words, sentences, characters, or situations in Foote's early fiction emphasize his independence by their rarity. More fundamentally, he took a distinguishable approach in narrative construction—not that he did not profit by lessons learned from Faulkner, as he has freely admitted. He also saw Jordan County, with its urban and industrial northern part and its agrarian southern section, as a microcosm of the United States and not so idiosyncratically Southern as Yoknapatawpha.

## Tournament

Shelby Foote's first novel was *Tournament,* published by the Dial Press in 1949. In an interview with Evans Harrington, Foote discussed its genesis and its qualities with humor but also with affection for the rich little book that he recognizes as "certainly . . . a first novel." In 1939, Foote "protested" Hitler's invasion of Poland by joining the Mississippi National Guard, and in the year before it was mobilized he wrote the first version of his first novel and sent it to Alfred A. Knopf. The well-known editor Harold Strauss was impressed by it, saw its faults, and gave the young author advice which he appreciated and more or less followed: "put it away, go on and write the next one." After his war service, Foote took the five-year-old manuscript "out of the closet," saw that Strauss had been right but that there were good parts too, rewrote it, and kept on writing. He spoke of the revision as "a discovering that maybe I could write. . . . I was thrashing around in the wilds in the English language . . . and looking at my homeland in a way I had never done before."[1]

*Tournament* concerns the precipitous rise and fall of Hugh Bart, a planter who settles in the Delta after the Civil War. The story is told by his grandson, Asa, who seeks to understand how and why the grandfather was able to restore Solitaire, a baronial plantation on Lake Jordan which was sacked during the war, only to fail as husband and father, sell the land when his sons proved incompetent to manage it, and finally to lose his fortune through imprudent investment and gambling. An arriviste in Jordan County, Bart marries the daughter of General Jameson, "the Delta's beau sabreur" of Civil War renown who had inherited Solitaire from his father, Isaac, a pioneer settler. Bart acquires the plantation after the impoverished Jamesons have lost it and seeks ambivalently to redeem the old order by installing the Jameson daughter as chatelaine. Isaac, the General, and Bart, although each has come to grief one way or another at Solitaire, loom heroically by comparison with Asa's feckless father and Asa himself.

As Asa grows up, he is discomfited and puzzled by the paltriness of the family's circumstances in Bristol and the sharp contrast they make with the recent yet mythic past at Solitaire. He suspects the explanation lies in the character and fate of Hugh Bart, which he investigates. Asa's point of view, although not specifically invoked again in the later Jordan County works, may be said to condition all of them. It is the point of view of the author's generation, and it is autobiographical to a degree which has evidently influenced his decision to keep *Tournament* out of print and use it as a storehouse of Jordan County materials.

The pattern of family history exemplified by the Bart-Jameson clan is a background theme developed in various ways in all of the Jordan County group. In *Tournament* and subsequent works Foote deals with a related theme, the thinness and inauthenticity of Delta culture, interwoven with another preoccupation, the relationships of fathers, father-substitutes, and children. The latter always suffer from deprivation stemming from male and paternal inadequacies. The testing of men and attainment of male *virtù,* typically through violence and especially war, and its dissipation are of central importance.[2] Also recurrent although only suggested by the figure of Asa Bart is the "portrait of the artist," often the potential artist who is balked or fails.

Subsuming all of these is the grand theme which Asa announces and which recurs throughout Foote's work: the loneliness of the human condition and the inherent difficulty of building any kind of satisfactory life at all. Asa Bart, having reconstructed the life of his grandfather, comes to this grim conclusion:

> And though I know now there is no call for reproach or even regret, there was a time when I cursed him for a ruthless man; I thought that, like others of his improvident generation, Bart had thrown away the land and money which would have made my life so different and, I thought, better. By the time I was old enough to begin to learn what really had happened, however, I was too overwhelmed, too much like a man looking down into an abyss, for there to be room for anything but terror: I was heartsick. This is expiation. Men stand alone; they earn their fates. (xvi)[3]

Asa arrives at a mature and therefore charitable attitude toward his grandfather. Resentment of the grandfather's failings and, implicitly, of the effect of these in having made the father less of a man than he might have been, has been resolved in a disabused recognition of a plain fact about the human condition in general. Sins of omission as well as commission there had certainly been, some quite particular to the Delta

and the given family situation; but Asa transcends the latter sufficiently
to see it and the homeland that shaped it in proportion—as an artist
might. He is finally capable of sympathy, as one man to another, with
his grandfather. His vivid memory of his grandfather's death ends the
novel: "He lay there motionless, calm, his hands outside the covers, his
head on a pillow, the mustache dark brown and exact, his lips moving
beneath it. 'The four walls are gone from around me, the roof from over
my head. I'm in the dark, alone'" (xviii).

Answering a question by Harrington about how he "came upon" the
vivid character of Hugh Bart, Foote replied, "He is based on my notion
of my grandfather [Huger Lee Foote], who died about two years before I
was born." He added that he had "seen men more or less like him" and
based the character on knowledge and observation of "many men . . .
over the years," holding firmly to the belief that character creates the
situation, not otherwise.[4]

Extending the pattern of family rise and fall—strength in an elder
generation followed in the younger ones by weakness, ineffectualness,
or fecklessness—are several miniature stories which supplement or
underscore the Bart-Jameson story. The Tarfellers, for example, who
live on a neighboring plantation, are headed by a father who sits and
drinks and is finally shot down in a confrontation with his daughter's
lover which is a bizarre mixture of the comic and tragic. Kate Bateman,
the "wild," impulsive girl who marries Hugh Bart, Jr., is "high-born,
or at least what they called high-born: her great-grandfather had been
one of the founders." Her grandfather, however, "lost most of the
family money and land, mismanaging and gambling them away," and
her father operates a cotton office in town "from within a sort of
alcoholic lambency" (159, 163).

*Tournament* is very consciously structured, with a carefully varied interplay of points of view and a design analogous in some respects to music. It begins with an "overture" in Asa Bart's first person, recounting
his birth at Solitaire in November, the "autumn days," in the words of
one of Foote's favorite poets, that "are the most used-up thing on
earth."[5] The place shows signs of neglect. Hugh Bart, off trapshooting
in Kentucky, has lost the will to make it thrive. The leaves are "sodden
and viscid underfoot, each a small death." The plantation bell is
"deadened by the rain," the lake is "shrouded," the walls are "sweating
drops like tears," and the plaster is falling (ix). Foote modulates into
omniscience for the body of the novel and then moves back to Asa for

the concluding commentary or "coda." This begins with Hugh Bart's funeral and is interspersed with flashes of memory of his last hours, the later death of his son—Asa's father—and the young man's troubled thoughts about his own changing attitudes and search for meanings.

Asa reports that he only gradually learned the full story, which "was formed as mudflats are formed on the river, layer by layer brought grain by grain by the shifting current, the tricky boils and eddies. . . ." He first hears the story of Hugh Bart's last years from his grandfather's faithful Billy Boy, a poor white living "on a place adjoining a portion of what used to be Solitaire." Faintly reminiscent of Wash Jones in his relationship with Colonel Sutpen, Billy Boy has, however, his own character and is used for different ends. In his eyes, Bart was a "proud tall figure" who "cast his shadow, immense and knightly and biblical in the rich, unreal glare of hero-worship" (xiv, xi, xiii)—a figure bringing to mind the monument to LeRoy Percy.

This reference to Bart as "knightly"—unless his name is meant to be read so—is the one explicit allusion to the complex of meanings, most of them ironic, which the title of the novel is intended to convey. Although Foote has explained that there were actual tournaments at Lake Washington in the early days (see Allen Tate's novel *The Fathers* for a rendition of the doubtless more elaborate Virginia examples), the tournament of the title is of course metaphorical. It refers first to Bart's career, his successive jousts with people and circumstances, and also to the theme of Delta culture and its unconvincing imitation of Virginia.[6] A tournament as enjoyed by Isaac Jameson and his friends might feature a brawny Negro butting heads with a bull.

The novel proper, dealing with Hugh Bart's career, comprises eight sections, meticulously deployed and balanced. The first two are devoted to Bart's rise and acquisition of Solitaire, so named by the founder, Isaac Jameson, who had thought he would never marry. Bart, too, is a bachelor when he buys the place. Although he marries and fathers a family, the relationships fail. Solitaire figures in several subsequent works, most notably in one of the finest of Foote's stories, "Pillar of Fire" in *Jordan County,* gathering symbolic value through its repeated appearances.

The four middle sections are devoted to Hugh Bart's increasingly effective management of the estate even as he undercuts the enterprise by his incapacity for sustained commitment, which leads to ennui, demoralization, and sale of the land. A man of boundlesss energy, "born for work and risk," he nevertheless fulfills a prophecy by his friend and substitute father, Judge Wiltner: he must go on, he "cant [*sic*] loaf on a slope."[7] If he chooses the wrong way, he will "snarl up the whole business . . . undo in a hurry" all that he has accomplished. " 'Youll bungle, son,' " the Judge tells him, " 'youll bungle. Youll die with the whole thing gone crash in your lap' "(53).

Successful but increasingly bored, Bart turns to hunting—he evidently has no intellectual interests. Spectacularly successful as a hunter, he seeks the more artificial excitement of trapshooting in state, regional, and national contests. He begins to drink, and his health begins to fail. In the meantime, his children are strangers: Solitaire was rightly named. The first son is lost, ineffectual; the daughter, a lesbian given to literary pursuits; the third child, a son, is too easily successful but accident-prone, a mama's boy, an escapist.

The two-chapter opening of Hugh Bart's story ends upon a note that will echo through the rest of his career and through Foote's later fiction. Having borrowed to buy Solitaire, Bart is well along toward retiring the mortgage when the banker in Ithaca, Lawrence Tilden—whose son will figure in a later novel—persuades him to lend money to "a merchant in Bristol" (55) who wishes to expand his dry-goods store. The merchant is a Jew from Austria and so reminds us of the novelist's maternal grandfather. The importance of the material to the novelist and his conception of the Delta is suggested by this circumstance and by his adapting it for publication, prior to that of *Tournament,* as a small book published in Greenville under the title *The Merchant of Bristol.*

The allusion to Shylock signals, in an ironic way, money as a theme of the Jordan County fictions. The sympathetically presented merchant cannot pay his note on time, is cruelly and avariciously refused an extension by the banker, and commits suicide. While in effect counting on the suicide, the banker arranges the purchase of the dry-goods store at an extra profit for the bank and Bart. On learning the circumstances, Bart is outraged: "It was the beginning of the antagonism he was to feel for all who made their livelihoods by the manipulation of nothing but money" (54).

An exciting part of the main body of the novel comes in the section called "The River," concerning the Mississippi River flood of 1903. From this section, as we have indicated, the author's first published story was adapted. With the aid of some Negroes, Bart attempts to rescue a neighbor, finds him dead, and buries him in the water among cedar tops marking the cemetery. The episode comes just before Bart, finding "no object on which to expend the energy, allay the ache" (117–18), realizes that his son cannot and will not manage and hold Solitaire and announces to his stricken but silent wife that he is selling her ancestral home. The baby Asa can be heard wailing in a farther room.

The last two sections concern Hugh Bart's life in a rapidly changing Bristol under the sign of the dollar. The point has not yet been spelled out in Foote's fiction, but the implication first and last seems to be that—to recall John Faulkner's phrase—"dollar cotton" is a fatal variety and leads to ever more unfortunate involvement with the cash nexus. Bart invests the proceeds of the sale of Solitaire, and the investment proves disastrous. Meanwhile, Bart takes up "unvarnished" gambling (investment apparently is regarded as a varnished kind) in the smoky Inferno of the Elks Club. He drinks more, and his health breaks at the same time that the Memphis bank which manages his money fails. He then gambles suicidally, not for pleasure but for profit, and his wife and children come to their various personal disasters, which seem to be functions of his own.

### Follow Me Down

*Follow Me Down* (1950) is full of cross-references to *Tournament* although these are not stressed but matter-of-fact and incidental to a very different and self-contained narrative. For this, the second of his novels to be published, but written after *Shiloh,* Foote turned to a different class, a different time, but the place is Jordan County. The novel concerns Luther Eustis, a severely repressed, fanatically fundamentalist farmer working land that was part of Solitaire. The name of the plantation resonates. It announces and summarizes the theme of alienation in *Tournament.* Now in *Follow Me Down* the poor white Eustises inherit the consequences of what is stated by the most sophisticated character in the novel to be "the failure of Love," just as the descendants of Hugh Bart do.

On a summer's day in 1949, Luther Eustis, seized by passion for the young country whore Beulah Ross, abandons his family and takes the girl to an island in a lake formed from the Mississippi River where, after an Edenic interlude, he drowns her. The design comprises multiple points of view, none definitive, all needed for an adequate account of Eustis's "truly complicated" crime and punishment. Compared with *Tournament,* carefully constructed though that is, *Follow Me Down* shows a marked gain in authority and control of the design of the novel. This should be appreciated by further comparison with the intervening work in *Shiloh,* which we have chosen to discuss hereafter as prologue to discussion of *The Civil War*; taken in order of composition, *Tournament, Shiloh,* and *Follow Me Down* reveal steady development in narrative skill.

The title *Follow Me Down* is taken from Leadbelly's (Huddie Ledbetter's) "Fannin Street," with its reiterated instruction, "follow me down," and prediction of destruction by the women there. Foote is also saying, "Follow *me* down"—into the lives of these characters, through events as I shall narrate; follow *them* down to experience "how it was" in depths of irrational religion, lust, cupidity, revenge, love, and pity; and so know all that happened in a way that no one character could know. Moreover, "following," in a variety of ways examined below, is a motif in the novel.

Presented in a richer, more complicated, and much better integrated form than the theme of *Tournament,* the major theme of *Follow Me Down* remains the same: the essential loneliness and difficulty of the human condition, as mediated by the Delta. This derives from evil in man and society and, seemingly, in the structure of the universe and is the cause as well as the effect of the failure of Love. James E. Kibler, Jr., emphasizing Foote's debt to literary naturalism, states that "the novel deals with the possibilities of moral choice in a world ordered by a merciless and inscrutable fate." He quotes Foote's assertion that "he made practically everyone in the book a victim of circumstances in one way or another, . . . and I remember I was trying to stress the valiance of practically everyone on earth in being able to get through life at all.' It is about 'the terrible sadness of life, the tragedy of it.'"[8]

The Eustises belong to the poor whites, one of three major classes that make up the population of the Delta. They are narrowly and emotionally religious and attest their conversions noisily. Literal minded in their application of the Bible, they are led by aggressive preachers, here, Brother Jimson, a bull of a man rampant in his pulpit. The old-fashioned religious view of the world held by Luther Eustis and his kind is played against the amorality of Beulah and her friends; and in monologues by persons of various shades of belief and disbelief a number of cross-lights illuminate the central situation. Observing that the "Old Testament sense of the unfathomable relation between man and his sins, his deserts, his ultimate fate" is a major concern of this novel, Walter Sullivan states that "Eustis himself is a man of God in the old sense—a monstrous sinner, like David or Jacob, bound by some terrible and mystic affection to the Almighty."[9]

Luther Eustis is the grandson of Luther Dade, who as a seventeen-year-old boy from Solitaire loses an arm in an affecting episode in *Shiloh.* As a stalwart old veteran, Dade had taken his namesake to a Confederate reunion on the island with which Luther Eustis therefore has meaningful associations and chooses for his Eden. For a while before his death, the old man had cared for his grandson after the murderous, fiery ending of the marriage of the younger Luther's promiscuous mother and half-crazed father. Kate, Luther Eustis's wife, who reveals most about his background, repeats that his heritage is "lust and murder."

His life has been harsh; and his marriage to Kate, who has loved him from childhood, is stale and unpromising. Whatever her good qualities—and they emerge numerous and important—she is lank and unappealing. The son for whom Luther longs is born dead, and then he begets the idiot Luty Pearl. For this child he bears a special burden of grief. His eldest daughter has her sexuality diverted into a early marriage. The unattractive second daughter is an old maid, bitter and rebellious against labor and deprivation. At fifty-one, Luther, who had undergone an explosive conversion after the birth of the "natural," turns more and more to biblical passages for guidance. He sees nothing ahead but a prospect of forever carrying Luty Pearl upstairs to bed as she sobs against his neck and, once there, having to adjust her chastity belt to prevent masturbation. So from his first sight of the amoral Beulah, Luther is caught in a vortex of passion which he can judge only as mortal sin.

Foote has commented in connection with this novel, "I like to get out the same way I got in."[10] He gets in—that is, approaches the central situation of Luther and Beulah—through successively more personally involved characters delivering monologues. The novel contains three parts, each of which is comprised of three monologues, with a variation in the second part. In Part I, the opening voice is that of the circuit court clerk, who has only a functionary's interest in Luther's trial for murder; the next is that of Stevenson, a newspaper reporter, who has a limited professional interest; and the third is that of Dummy, an afflicted boy who has been on the island with Eustis and Beulah, felt desire for her, and in his grief and frustration at her death informed the sheriff that Eustis had killed her.

Part II, the longest, is presented through Eustis in three sections, followed by Beulah in one section, and then Eustis again in three sections. The crime, what led to it, and what followed it emerge through the consciousness of the murderer and the victim. The reader thus possesses more of the truth of it than any of the characters—including the principals.

Then in Part III Foote "gets out" via monologues reversing the emphasis in Part I. The progression is through an intimately affected person (Eustis's wife, Kate, whose monologue balances that of Dummy, whose passionate attachment was to Beulah); through another professional (Eustis's defense lawyer, Parker Nowell, who balances the reporter); and finally through another functionary (the turnkey of the county jail, who balances the circuit court clerk). Only the central monologues of Eustis and Beulah are presented under proper names. The others, information about the speakers of which emerges in seemingly casual ways in other monologues, are identified by function or attribute. The effect upon the reader is that of intensifying involvement in the passion of Luther Eustis, culminating in identification with the two principals, followed by gradual withdrawal to the social perspective imbued, however, with humane sympathy which has been generated by the narrative.

Foote not only moves in and out in this way but also backward and forward in time. The "immediate present" is the first week in September 1949, specifically the last day of Eustis's trial. The first monologue begins and ends with the forenoon, and the last takes place in the late afternoon. There are other centers of interest, especially the finding of Beulah's body two months earlier, in late June, and the murder itself on June 21. As details are filled in by the speakers, the centers shift and the time perspective stretches back before the birth of Luther Eustis shortly before the turn of the century, overlapping the end of *Tournament*.

Foote has created a ninth major character who is not assigned a monologue but developed through appearances in all but one of the monologues. The patterning in threes is thus preserved despite the variation in Part II where Eustis is given two monologues. The character in question, Miz Pitts, is the mother of Dummy. She is a female instance of the failure of love grimmer, if possible, than the male instance of Eustis, with whom she feels an affinity. She tells him that she was a country schoolteacher and that her husband deserted her after a hysterectomy turned her into a "man." Her son, who functions as a parallel with Luty Pearl, was born mute and subsequently deafened by meningitis. Rendered grotesque in appearance and unable to bear the curiosity, gossip, and pity of her Alabama town, she has fled to the island where she ekes out a living by fishing and raising vegetables. She takes Eustis and Beulah to the island, guesses their secret, and finds the fish-eaten body of the girl when it rises in spite of the concrete blocks Eustis wired about the neck.

A careful reader of Browning, Foote has stated several times that he had *The Ring and the Book* in mind in structuring *Follow Me Down*; and he has also acknowledged his debt as monologuist to *The Sound and the Fury* and *As I Lay Dying*.[11] Little by little, the story is outlined, enlarged, modified, complicated, seen from various perspectives and from within participants, and finally distanced. The expansion and deepening continue through the quiet but powerful close. All the characters are implicated in different ways as voice after voice takes up the story to reveal a part, provide new information, and add something of its own. The scene is filled in; background and history are solidified. The reader follows, increasingly involved as the story emerges, the characters take on roundness, and the several themes combine into the major theme.

Before briefly considering the monologuists in the order of their appearance—since that order is crucial to the development of the narrative—we should point out a special structural effect Foote obtains through the monologue of the lawyer, Parker Nowell. This is the character who, on the basis of his own experience as well as observation of Eustis and the rest, can generalize: "Love has failed us. We are essentially, irrevocably alone. Anything that seems to combat that loneliness is a trap—Love is a trap: Love has failed us in this century. We left our better destiny in '65, defeated though we fought with a fury that seems to indicate foreknowledge of what would follow if we lost. Probably it happened even earlier: maybe in Jackson's time. Anyhow—whenever—we left the wellsprings, and ever since then we have been moving toward this ultimate failure of nerve."[12]

Nowell begins and ends with allusions to Mozart and Beethoven, his passion and solace being music. He shapes his closing argument in Eustis's defense in "sonata-form: Exposition, Development, Recapitulation" (253). The result is a review in musical terms of the whole tripartite novel. Foote, who himself knows and loves music, the jazz of the Delta, its folk songs, and popular songs as well as classical music, employs it allusively and structurally throughout his work, including *The Civil War.* In this he has gone to school to James Joyce and, among Americans, F. Scott Fitzgerald and others. Walter Sullivan finds that "Nowell is defined in terms of music which is formal but amoral, as is his life."[13] But Nowell immediately finds his own sonata analogy highfalutin in the circumstances and adds that he will give the jurors a closing argument in the plainer army way of telling 'em what you're going to tell 'em, telling 'em, and then telling 'em what you have already told 'em.

The monologues are all basically realistic. Each reveals the character of the speaker and provides his or her slant on the scene; and each carries forward the tightly woven plot, beginning quick on a high point of action and moving forward to end on a note of suspense. The monologue of the circuit court clerk opens the "Exposition." A tall, lean hanger-on around the courthouse, he begins with a fast-paced account of Eustis's trial in September under Judge Holiman, a hanging judge, but retraces events from the discovery of Beulah's body in late June. What he has to say is part of the gossip of the courthouse gang as they discuss happenings in the courtroom up to the time the jury files out to consider its verdict.

The newspaper reporter follows with a longer, two-section monologue which covers four days at the end of June and fills in details from the day the body is found until he surmises Parker Nowell is taking Eustis's case. The reporter's interest is somewhat venal, but his story is accurate although vivified to suit his prejudices and purposes. He hopes to sell it to *Real Detective.* He has a callow, jaundiced opinion of most of his fellow townsmen although he is capable of sympathy with the effeminate photographer who must photograph the sickening corpse. He touches two of the governing analogues; in an interview with Eustis, he suddenly thinks of Milton's Satan, and he sees that the Adam and Eve analogue works—to a point. Through him the reader gets the public view.

Miz Pitts's son James Elmo, called Dummy by all, is given the concluding monologue in the "Exposition." Round-headed and silly-looking and taken to be dumb in several senses, he is unexpectedly literate, reads lips, and finds his outlet in studying the dictionary and practicing the beautiful script through which he communicates. Beulah dominates his narrative, which starts with his realization that Eustis has killed his beloved "Sue"—as Beulah was known on the island—and his determination to venture out alone to reveal what he knows. He goes back in time to cover intensively the slightly more than two weeks the lovers have spent on the island. Smitten by Beulah, he hangs around her and watches her making love with Eustis in the role of a voyeur, a role that will reappear in Foote's later stories. His desire becomes agonizing. After Eustis kills the girl, Dummy makes an excruciating trip to Bristol, "following" Beulah in his dream on the way, to give the sheriff a note identifying the murderer. Ironically, the Bible betrays Eustis to Dummy although Eustis, like Beulah, used a false name. He had taken his Bible as well as the girl with him, and Dummy has seen his correct name and the name of Solitaire on the flyleaf. This is an especially effective recurrence of the symbolic effect of the old plantation.

The two monologues by Luther Eustis frame the central monologue by Beulah. The three comprise the "Development" and present the inside views of the crime, Eustis's played against Beulah's, both against the views that precede and follow. Eustis's first monologue, divided into three sections, covers his thoughts and actions from his first sight of the girl—when she and a friend out with two soldiers scandalously break up an outdoor preaching Eustis is attending—through his last sight of her face as he strangles and drowns her. In his second monologue, also in three sections, he gives his account of his flight from the island to Bristol, his brief sojourn in what he sees as the inferno of the city, and his return to Solitaire.

The reader feels distress that grows as he follows Eustis's earnest, spare recital laced with biblical echoes, allusions, and quotations through the terrible events, always accompanied by if not actually caused by Eustis's increasingly violent spiritual struggles. His contest, whatever its outcome, may result in his conviction of damnation but cannot shake his faith in God. He could say with Job, "Though he slay me, yet will I trust in him."

These central monologues exemplify Foote's increasing virtuosity in employing the form from novel to novel. The action moves rapidly, the flashbacks that fill in the background are economical and cogent, the psychological entanglements and struggles intensify to the breaking point at the end of each division. The language is right for the

characters in idiom, syntax, and allocation of figures. Eustis's torment
from his initial view of Beulah in firelight as she comes out of the bushes
straightening her skirt develops into a conviction that God commands
him to *"teach her what it means to be a Christian"* even though he must
*"bow down to the flesh"* to do so (93). She, attracted by his passion, makes
herself available.

In the second section of his first monologue, flashback is effectively
used. On the island with Beulah, Eustis recalls the childhood visit he
made to it with his grandfather Luther Dade, thinking of it as "the
Garden . . . before the Serpent sneaked in and corrupted it" (97). But
he knows and soon compulsively shows that the Serpent is present.
Inevitably—as the reader feels—he comes to see the Serpent in the
guise of his nineteen-year-old girl and so announces starkly at the
beginning of the third section of his first monologue, "I have to go
back."

The struggle with Beulah is short but intense, only a climactic
episode in his prolonged struggle with himself and God. He concludes
that God is saying, *"I'll leave it to you."* Beulah having innocently asked
his permission to serve poor famished Dummy since otherwise he will
"go through life . . . not knowing," Eustis cannot doubt that she is "all
the way depraved." She is Jezebel. In the willow-screened cove where
they swim, he strangles her with willow switches, forcing her down
into the water even though "an evil woman is smoother than oil" (123,
115, 124).

Eustis's second monologue begins with his version of the Mississippi
levee area as wilderness. His dreams and increasingly anguished
thoughts are presented altogether in biblical terms. In dreams he
wrestles like Jacob with an angel that turns out to be an avenging
Beulah. God questions him as to whether or not he would, in his
extreme hunger, have murdered two Negro women whom he encounters for the fish they had caught. He is fighting off the realization that
he is Ishmael, with his hand raised against every man and threatened by
every man in turn, when on the third night after the crime he makes his
way out of the wilderness toward Bristol. He sees the lights "rose-
yellow, like the fires of hell" in the city of sin (153).

Foote presents through the eyes of this man born and bred in the
country and committed to the old faith the seamy quarters of mid-
century Bristol. In a café where customs and speech are as foreign to
him as the music that blares from a juke box, "Civilization" is the name

of the selection that puzzles him most. Spending the night in a flophouse beside a diseased old drunkard who intends to rob him, Eustis is tempted to murder again; but no voice comes from God and he refrains.

In the section devoted to his return by train to Ithaca, the village near Solitaire, he changes into clothes bought at a salvage store where he tells the clerk his name is Legion. After a bath and shave in a barber shop he thinks that he has been spiritually cleansed as well. He says, "Then I went out—like Legion in the Bible, fully dressed and in my right mind again." He is engaging in magical thinking to undo his deed. Beulah is everywhere, and he hears her speak. In his pathetic reunion with his family, Luty Pearl rejects him and the mechanical ducks he has brought her from Bristol. He cannot go to church, knowing at last the extent of his own evil: "God would strike me dead," he reflects, "for bringing Satan into the house of prayer" (179, 193). He sits, waiting for whatever God may send.

Beulah's short monologue at the center of the novel is more stylized than the others. Represented as occurring in a timeless present as she drowns, it is handled in much the same way as Addie Bundren's in *As I Lay Dying.* The reader actually follows her down into the water, "the bubbles trailing upward, pearls on a string" (125). The girl, who reveals that she is pregnant but has not told Eustis, takes up her story at the time of the Easter picnic when she first came to his notice. She relives the squalid years during which her mother used her as "a stalking horse" for men. Ignorant, pathetic, but with sex appeal sufficiently compelling in her time and place, she prides herself on being "steadfast" to Eustis. He is finally "the right man" she had not found through numerous previous adventures.

The motif of "following" centers in her, in her own monologue as well as in those of Eustis and Dummy. Her insistence that she will "follow" and "knock at the door" when Eustis declares that he must return to his family precipitates the murder: "I'll follow. . . . I will. I'll follow you wherever. I don't want a life with you not there" (119). And indeed she does follow, usually in biblical disguises in Eustis's nightmares as well as in his waking thoughts which at times, as on the train, reach the quality of hallucination.

Her ideas about the situation are revealed as she worries. The motif "something is going to happen" is recurrent: "That Dummy, I thought—exasperated; it's what I get for trying to do good" (142, 143).

Her innocent tone plays against the ways she is seen by other characters variously as merely a sex object, a victim, or an embodiment of evil. Nowell sees her as a product of her heritage and environment, especially of her mother's evil, not her own, and asserts that it is the mother and not Eustis who should be on trial.

Kate Eustis's straightforward account, as different as possible from Beulah's, opens the "Recapitulation," balancing Dummy's at the close of the "Exposition" by her love for Eustis as opposed to Dummy's attachment to Beulah. Language and syntax are right for the hard-working, long-suffering country woman. Kate conveys the story of her husband's family and his life up to the time of his return from the island and arrest. She endures what life brings her and remains loyal to the man she has loved and understood since his tragic boyhood, whose fate she has foreseen "as a straight path."

When Eustis returns, Kate is steadfast, with an awkward dignity and faith which impress even the most skeptical and callous of the other persons involved. Asked by Nowell when she is on the witness stand whether she has forgiven Eustis, she replies, "I never forgive him, for I never felt it was anything that called to be forgiven. I never blamed him. I knew in my heart, whatever was done, it was the other Him that did it, not the one thats here on trial" (245). Her fundamental sympathy for her man, in terms of the religious context and ethos that she shares with him, emerges in this parallel with his own view of himself as Legion.

We have had occasion to say something of the monologue by the lawyer, Parker Nowell, which is the central element of what this character himself thinks of as the "Recapitulation." As Eustis's attorney, he is the recipient of what everybody concerned with the crime has to say and thus has more than anybody else to reflect on. There is a heightened effect as compared with that of the balancing monologue in the "Exposition" by the reporter Stevenson. Both are only professionally involved, but Nowell is professionally committed to Eustis's welfare and so more deeply affected than the reporter who has only to retail events. Knowledgeable though he is, Nowell at the end of the trial can only await the jury's verdict like everyone else, and his monologue, too, closes on a suspenseful note.

He looks at his stoical client, for whom the prosecuting attorney wants death, for whom he himself wants "something less"—but "The jury—what did they want?" Nowell feels that he has done his best, "sonata-form closing argument and all," but he cannot be sure of his effect. He hums the molto adagio from the *Heiliger Dankgesang,* Foote obligingly quoting the musical notation, knowing that there are those to whom even this "would be no more than noise; theyd squirm to hear it" (254).

The closing monologue, by Roscoe Jeffcoat, turnkey of the county jail, opens with the speaker much upset because his duties, which he performs not without complaint, have prevented his learning the verdict. He catches up, as he catches up quickly enough on everything that goes on: Eustis has been sentenced to life imprisonment at Parchman, the legendary Mississippi prison farm in the northern part of the Delta.

Garrulous Roscoe gets "lonesome in that jail." A big man, gossipy and crude, he is also observant and, in a rough-hewn way, thoughtful and sympathetic. Cooped up in an apartment in the jail building with his wife who is self-conscious, jealous, and shrewish because of a goiter, this functionary performs his onerous duties well. While trying to know and tell all, he eases the plight of the prisoners as best he can. He picks up strands from various stories and ties them neatly, gossiping about circumstances and lending substance and plausibility to the narrative. From him come details about characters who have appeared in the novel and left the reader wondering, for example, about the reporter's disappointment when an older reporter has "scooped" him and sold the story of Eustis's crime to a magazine. Roscoe Jeffcoat likes a story and likes it complete; all the while he talks, he contributes to the denouement of Luther Eustis's story.

When he learns the verdict, the turnkey tries to make it easier for Eustis by explaining how and when he will go to Parchman and what life is like there: "It aint so bad, considering"; for the "Midnight Special," that train celebrated in song by Leadbelly and so suggesting a balance with the title of the novel, brings the women to visit once a month (268–69). Trudging up and down a spiral stair to lock up prisoners, take visitors up, and feed his charges, Jeffcoat ponders justice, human relationships, and the order of things. He supplies data and arrives at insights that would surprise the elegant Nowell, for example, and the reader is accordingly alerted to the circumstance that there's more to Jordan County than can be wrapped up in sonata form.

Jeffcoat provides the report of the visit to Eustis's cell made following the end of the trial by Kate, the couple's eldest daughter and her husband, and Brother Jimson the family preacher. Though he draws distinctions between country and city ways, Jeffcoat admits he was "a country boy" himself. He gives a surprisingly delicate account of the wordless reconciliation between Kate and Eustis—"I turned my head," he says; "it didnt seem right to watch. . . . " Brother Jimson leads the group in prayer "loud and strong." Jeffcoat notes this circumstance but adds, "I knelt too, finally; it didnt seem right not to." Almost alone in the book, he can recognize and ponder Eustis's attractiveness to women: Kate, Beulah—and Miz Pitts, who brings him sweet potato pies in jail. They come in "a round tin plate with a freshly laundered square of cloth on top, sugar-sack material bleached white, the creases still sharp where she'd ironed it on the island" (265, 266, 270). Turnkey gets his taste but is obviously moved as well as baffled.

His monologue makes an artful close, conveying, through a character and a sensibility that might themselves require special insight to be seen as sympathetic, a humane view of the principals and other characters. Worn out from his trips up and down, his corns killing him, stout Jeffcoat feels sorry for himself but can spare a little concern for Eustis as he waits for "the long-chain man." This is a term carried over from the days when an officer escorted prisoners to Parchman on the train instead of in the van, looking like a school bus, which has replaced it. The prisoners were manacled to a chain running the length of the car, and Jeffcoat's mentioning that chain reminds the reader of poor Beulah's golden one clasped around her ankle, asserting love.

## Chapter Three

# The Jordan County Story Continues: *Love in a Dry Season*

Foote has said that *Love in a Dry Season* (1951) is "a great favorite" of his if "not *the* favorite all the time" among his books, explaining that he likes it "because of a sort of happy facility I had during the writing of it." He remembers the experience "with great affection." His feeling "has nothing to do with the worth of the book." Simply, it made him "happy," and he "thought it was a funny book."[1] Having dealt with the failures of love among the poor whites of modern Jordan County in *Follow Me Down,* he extended this theme to "the quality" in a comic novel with cutting edges. There is a marked change in method and especially in tone from the previous novels. The author shifts from reliance upon interior monologue, designed to arouse sympathy with even the most outré characters, to a modified omniscience which delivers a mordant judgment.

Foote states that he took the title from Dryden's translation of Virgil's First Georgic: "Linseed and fruitful poppy bury warm,/In a dry season, and prevent the storm./Sow beans and clover in a rotten soil."[2] This is the Georgic, "concerned with plowing, sowing and the weather signs," that is closest in spirit to Hesiod's *Works and Days.*[3] But because of its subject matter and tone Foote's novel also brings to mind "the dry season" of T. S. Eliot's "Gerontion"—a season of decay and despair. Like other titles and epigraphs used by Foote, *Love in a Dry Season* is in part denotative and specifically descriptive of his theme and in part atmospheric, connotative. The reader who finds out the source is tempted to tease out implications. For example, there may be a hidden play on "prevent" in the sense of "to anticipate" or "precede"; the novel ends in storms of scandal and gossip while in the world beyond Jordan County the storm of World War II rages, bringing further change, mostly in the direction of breakdown and alienation so far as Jordan

County is concerned. The soil, not "soft, yielding, or friable as the result of decomposition" making for richness and fruitfulness, is however "rotten" in other senses. The season is "dry" indeed, and the harvest represents a return only too appropriate on what has been sown, in soil such as it is.

At any rate, to shift allusion slightly, *Love in a Dry Season* presents Shelby Foote's wasteland. The main action occurs from 1928 to 1941, extended backward in the exposition to 1873 and forward to 1945 in a section that functions as an epilogue. Foote has stated that he was concerned with the Depression as a specifically "dry season." The degeneration of the upper class has rendered it vulnerable to the opportunism of an ousider, a midwesterner of immigrant stock with an Anglicized name, Harley Drew. He sets out to marry for her money a spinster, Amanda Barcroft, daughter of Major Barcroft, one of Jordan County's inadequate males, gone sour and snobbish, whose failed masculinity is a bane to his womenfolk. On thinking he sees a better opportunity in beautiful, wealthy Amy Carruthers, wife of the blind and impotent Jeff Carruthers and heiress of Briartree, a plantation near Solitaire, Drew abandons Amanda for Amy, with unexpected results.

Treating this double triangle with Harley Drew as the common element, the author again planned a complex, strongly articulated narrative meant to adumbrate a truth yet more "complicated" than that of the earlier novels.

The ingenious construction has received the pleased attention of Simone Vauthier, one of Foote's French critics, who dwells upon the "superimposition" of "ternary and binary patterns." These involve an interplay of voyeurs and their objects, inversions and reversals of roles, so that seeing and being seen, for lack of viable human relationships, become "one of the metaphorical centers" of the novel.[4] Drew weaves deviously in and out of the Barcroft plot and the Carruthers plot; but all the players are held in "the great 'Eye of Bristol,'" symbolized by the traffic light.

Within the enveloping theme of isolation, both the Barcrofts and the Carrutherses carry forward the theme of decline through the generations. War as the virtually indispensable means of proving men and men so proved as the indispensable resource of women are present as background themes. The war theme is given ironic twists and used as a metaphor throughout the novel. In the foreground is the war between the sexes presented in several variations, including female as killer and female as victim. Harley Drew, né Charles Drubashevski, son of a

Polish steel worker and a Scandinavian woman in Youngstown, Ohio—whose drabness he industriously flees—carries the theme of the outsider as a disturbing force in Jordan County. Part of the comedy comes from the reader's realizing that, if Drew had his reasons for escaping Youngstown, he did not know—poor Yankee—what he was getting into in Bristol.

Change, despite the all-American belief to the contrary, is apparently not progress, at least to any desirable goal, in Bristol and Jordan County. Changes from Reconstruction to World War I affected the characters and action of *Tournament*. They are implicit in the contrasts of *Follow Me Down*. In *Love in a Dry Season,* Bristol in the 1920s and 1930s is seen to be changing even more rapidly than in the past. The making and losing of fortunes is a theme extending from *Tournament* together with that of gambling. If Hugh Bart gambled, so does Harley Drew despite his more modern connotation as "speculator"—actual and metaphorical. The four great oaks in front of "the big gray house on Lamar Street" where the Barcrofts live (Foote gave this family his maternal grandfather's house and even gave the Major his grandfather's looks and bearing though nothing of his character) symbolize the change. One by one, three of them disappear, marking the decline of the family and the neighborhood. Finally, the house is demolished and replaced by a garage. One oak, called the Barcroft Oak, remains, girdled by a bench where "off-shift workers . . . sit . . . watching cars go by." It remains a landmark "even after most people no longer remembered how it got its name" (246).[5]

Working again with his "magical number three," Foote composed *Love in a Dry Season* in three parts each organized into three chapters. Part I introduces the Barcrofts, Jeff and Amy Carruthers, and Harley Drew; Part II covers Drew's campaigns first for Amanda, then for Amy; Part III resolves his effects in both camps and leaves Drew, Amanda, and Amy essentially unaffected. Each continues in his original mode: Harley Drew, abandoning Bristol as a lost cause, marries money in Memphis; Amy, abandoning Bristol, continues a luxurious, promiscuous, empty life; Amanda, remaining in Bristol, is the eccentric old maid everybody felt she must be from her youth up. If there is development in anyone, it is in Amanda, for she survives a cruel father and a false lover with dignity and seems content at the end.

The Barcrofts are shown from the first to be in a state of decline with the remaining male representative of the line having become an anachronism to the point of caricature. Prim, stiff, and formal, Major

Malcolm Barcroft is "an institution in Bristol, one of the final representatives of what the town had progressed beyond" (3). If Major Barcroft
is an absurd embodiment of tradition, Bristol has not moved on to
anything better. Major Barcroft's father was a Confederate officer who
lost an arm in war (like Luther Dade in the lower order) and then was
killed honorably "in a scuffle over a ballot box with one of Governor
Ames' imported election officials" during Reconstruction (4). The
orphaned Malcolm goes to military prep school and develops a fixation
on the Civil War as lasting as Uncle Toby's obsession with Namur in
Laurence Sterne's *Tristram Shandy*. He dreams of the military exploits
which will validate his manhood but has the opportunity to serve only
briefly in Florida during the Spanish-American War and is crushed at
being rejected for World War I because of a heart condition.

The would-be military hero restores the family fortunes, however, by
marrying the daughter of a wealthy planter. He in effect kills his wife in
his determination to beget a son after she has borne two daughters and a
third pregnancy is known to be dangerous to her. The reader may recall
the same obsession reflected in the lower order in the case of Luther
Eustis. The Major detests women, sadistically domineers over his
daughters, but gets his comeuppance in the effeminacy of his son,
whom he kills indirectly by forcing him to use guns. At eleven, the boy
is accidentally shot. At the time of the main action of the novel, the
Major is a cotton broker, reputed to be a millionaire, who lives
vicariously as "Cadet Captain Barcroft" and tyrannizes Amanda and
her invalid sister Florence. It develops, however, that he has invested
unwisely—Foote's Delta fatalities recur—and has little left of the
fortune Bristol and Harley Drew think he has. Most of this he wills to
his military school, leaving Amanda—her sister having died—a
pittance.

There is ambiguity as well as irony in the way the anonymous
narrator undercuts Major Barcroft's military preoccupations, for the
present is so rendered as to justify almost any form of dropping out and
it appears that even the Civil War heroes may or may not have been all
that they seem to their descendants. If there is a suggestion that war is
an outmoded way of proving manhood, it remains implicit and no
better way is developed.

A further overlay of irony on this theme is supplied by the circumstance that low-born Harley Drew, that avatar of the invading Yankee,
is a handsome man with military credentials that would have satisfied

Major Barcroft had he possessed them. Drew was awarded the DSC in World War I, during which he impressed his adjutant, Lawrence Tilden, another effeminate scion of the Jordan County upper class, who later gives Drew the job in his Bristol bank that allows the antihero to rise. Drew's military credentials are coin of the realm down South; for, though frustrated in Bristol, he is last seen as a social lion in Memphis, where he snares a rich wife, leading the debutante cotillion wearing "the uniform of a colonel in the Tennessee Home Guard" (250).

The Barcroft women are doomed. We know that the wife was sacrificed. Florence, the elder daughter, becomes an invalid recluse subject to nightmares in which her father attacks her, as he literally does in a grim scene when he supervises the cutting of her hair. Amanda, already fixed in the character of old maid, carries out the household duties with the help of Nora (mother of Duff Conway in the novella "Ride Out," which we discuss below), nurses the sister, attends the father. She is capable of at least a feeble bid for independence and what she imagines is love when Harley Drew comes to walk out with her in the shadows for his unworthy reasons and the Major opposes the marriage for unworthy reasons of his own. She feels bound to wait until her sister's impending death occurs to elope with Drew, but when the time comes, Drew, who awaits the Major's death, has seen Amy Carruthers and shifted his attack to a more lucrative and glamorous field.

Amanda saves the shreds of dignity after Drew, ludicrously defeated in his pursuit of Amy, has fled the field. Her small inheritance becomes adequate with changing times. For a while, she omnivorously reads novels about heroines that seem to have no relationship to her own story but gradually lives more through the newspapers, as her sister had done, and does war work with the ladies of her church circle, exchanging gossip and observing the life of the town. She who had been only watched as an object of curiosity and scandal, "she too became a watcher," the narrator comments as he brings the tale to a close. Amanda "had now herself become a part of the enormous eye, and was looking out as all those others had done" (248).

Amy and Jeff Carruthers are also decadent Southerners but of a different breed. He is an heir of a North Carolina tobacco fortune, and the couple is part of international café society. Amy has roots in Jordan County and inherits the dilapidated mansion and a portion of the land at Briartree through her aunt, Miss Bertha Tarfeller of *Tournament,* in which Bertha's affair with Downs Macready—another outsider, another gambler—ends in the deaths of both her feckless father and her lover. She appears also in *Follow Me Down* as the old-maid schoolteacher at Ithaca, another instance of a woman doomed by failed manhood in her family.

The Tarfellers of Briartree recapitulate the pattern which preoccupies Foote. The founder "had been a man of convictions and decisions, one of the original settlers"; described as "vapid and congenial," his son "had never done anything about anything"; Bertha paid the price; and now the family fetches up in the fourth generation with Amy. The family is beyond restoration, but the house at Briartree is not. By a sentimental caprice, Amy renders it "grander . . . than it had been in all its original glory . . . as sound as it had been back in '57 when it was built by the first Tarfeller. . . . 'They really knew how to build them in those days,'" the expensive architect engaged by the Carrutherses exclaims (26–27, 46). Amy's interest in Briartree evaporates, and the house is sold to the heirs of "the merchant of Bristol" whom we met in *Tournament*.

Foote has taken occasion to develop the characters of hardly any of the nineteenth-centry women of his Jordan County families, but he points out that Amy is not the kind of mistress Briartree had in the time of the founders. Amy is the unworthy "mistress, the chatelaine . . . successor to those other women, dead a generation now, who ran this house (and others like it, up and down the lake) with efficiency at hand like a muleskinner's whip, who wore clothes that gave inch for inch as much covering as armor and yet were able, laced and stayed as they were, not only to be willowy and tender but also to bear large numbers of children and raise them according to a formula whereby life was simple because indecision did not cloud it" (50; cf. *Tournament,* 36). Given such dams and sires as the early Tarfellers, it is not entirely clear, at least within *Love in a Dry Season,* how Jordan County has gone so far astray so soon.

Jeff Carruthers is a son of Josh Carruthers, a vigorous but self-indulgent man who married three women, the last an ex–chorus girl, in an apparent reference to the much-publicized Reynolds tobacco family's involvement with Libby Holman, the torch singer. His sons are lesser men than he as he is inferior to the strong father who founded the family fortune. The theme of family decline is thus repeated, this time among the Southern industrial rather than planter aristocracy. At Josh's funeral, the patriarch's portrait looks down, "mouth not so much cruel as

sardonic, the eyes clear blue." When the minister asserts that the nation
was built by such as Josh, "Amy believed for an instant that she saw the
portrait smile" (112, 113).

The novel's multiple play upon voyeurism reaches the extreme
combination of the literal and symbolic in Jeff Carruthers, a voyeur—a
practicing peeping Tom—who is blinded and who is, moreover,
homosexual. Amy, his cousin and his father's ward, has been promiscuous since age sixteen (the reader remembers Beulah Ross in the lower
order), and Jeff from thirteen her indulged "watcher." They grow up
inextricably entangled in a game of domination and subjection and
marry. Amy continues—as Jeff continues to enjoy watching—her
bouts with other men. However, driving recklessly in a fit of anger after
such an episode, he wrecks the car and, blinded, blames Amy. Thereafter their combat becomes "deadly." Amy can manage something like
sympathy: "For what could be more pitiful than a voyeur in the dark?"
(45). It is for the reader to infer that none of the characters is in much
better case.

After they restore Briartree, the couple travels abroad in luxury for
several years during which Amy philanders and Jeff reacts, even
shooting—but not to kill—at one of her lovers. He develops a consum-
ing interest in jazz, and he treasures his pistol: always the implication
that he might use it, but Amy does not think so. Growing bored in the
mid-1930s, Amy and Jeff return to Briartree to become the most
glamorous couple in Jordan County. They entertain lavishly and act
like visiting royalty in Bristol. Jeff, not even pathetic in his infantilism,
is now master of Briartree— "'Mars Jeff' he would have been called,
back in the days of the men he superseded, men who settled the land at
the time of Dancing Rabbit and worked it and built the houses
scattered along the cypress-screened shores of Lake Jordan, living their
lives with a singleness of purpose, save for the temporary distractions of
poker and hunting and whiskey, like priests whose cult was cotton"
(50; cf. *Tournament,* 36). The couple is ripe for entanglement with
Harley Drew, now vice president of the bank.

Harley Drew dominates the novel. In explaining once that he always
works from character in creating situation and not otherwise, Foote
used this character as example. Once conceived, he asserts, the character elaborates himself to a certain degree: "You put *a* man like Harley
Drew in *a* town like Bristol and things are going to happen; they're
going to naturally come about. He's going to be attracted to certain

women, he's going to be attracted to certain financial finaglings, he's going to come into contact with people who oppose him because they have a nature different from his, he's very apt to pursue some woman whose father disapproves—because what father wouldn't disapprove?"[6]

Traveling as representative of a St. Louis cotton broker, Drew is sent to Cotton Row in Bristol, where Major Barcroft is "the man to see." He also sees and decides to marry Amanda. Since this project will take time, he exploits his wartime acquaintance with Lawrence Tilden (there were also sexual overtones to his relationship with his St. Louis boss, and a species of infidelity is now involved) to get a job in Tilden's bank. Major Barcroft, whatever his own shortcomings, sees Drew for what he is and refuses to sanction the proposed marriage. He will disinherit Amanda if she marries against his wishes.

Forced into his waiting game, Drew courts Amanda secretly but "properly" at calculated intervals; he also receives whores at the hotel. He prudently gives up gambling, at which he has been adept since his army days, after being jarred into respect for "the best poker players in the world" (107) on the lower floor of the Elks Club (where not many years before Hugh Bart had not been prudent enough to stop). He places his bet rather on the Major's dying and leaving Amanda rich.

Preferring that all be smooth and easy, he really does not wish to be unkind but can be pushed to cruelty by his selfish interest. He strings Amanda along for years while setting his sights on Amy. When Amanda is ready, even to the packed trunk on the porch, to run away with him after her sister dies, he blurts that he won't marry her. For the Major lives, the will is therefore unexecuted, and Drew—though reluctant to close out such opportunity as Amanda may still represent—has transferred his ambition to Amy.

He has yet to learn how much Amy Carruthers outclasses him in selfishness and cruelty. He barely escapes with his life; but, as when he was outclassed at poker, he has the sense to cut his losses and run. He finds soon enough that his affair with her leads to frustration and gives her the upper hand. It does not make him master of Briartree. He cannot enjoy wealth, leisure, and the beautiful woman for all to see; it is a turn of the voyeur theme that others' seeing his enjoyment *is* his enjoyment.

Drew proposes to Amy that they murder Jeff; but the intended victim, more in love with Drew than Amy is, finally shoots Drew in the act of intercourse with her and smashes Amy's face with his pistol.

Recovering in the hospital, Drew speculates again on Amanda since the Major has died. When the contents of the Major's will are revealed and Amanda left poor, Drew sneaks out of town to begin a more successful campaign in Memphis. After the plastic surgeon provides Amy with a more expressionless beauty, she and Jeff drift from one fashionable spot to another, playing their deadly game just short of death. All three are in the public eye and so as happy as they are capable of being.

Bristol is vividly in the background of the two dramas. Harley Drew early realizes that "in Bristol everyone knew about everyone else—as if God, an enormous Eye in the sky, were telling secrets" (104). For much of the novel, the omniscient narrator focuses on the situation through Drew. He is in an adversary relation to the town, scornful, superior, yet envious and exceedingly cautious, wanting to become master of the Barcrofts' "big gray house on Lamar Street" or, better still, to be a latter-day "Mars Harley" of Briartree. Through Drew's casing the situation, the reader learns the business practices, the customs of the citizens who belong to the Kiwanis, the Rotary, and, at the top of the pecking order, the Country Club.

"Bristol's view" punctuates the narrative from time to time. Gossip, the "speculation" of the enormous Bristol eye, is constant. Bristol has peaks of excitement but tires quickly and creates its myths. For example, the townspeople know in general what Drew is about but come to feel kindly toward him and invent a "romance." The women flock to the Barcrofts' when Florence dies, "at once compassionate and prying, officious and perverse. . . ." The narrator makes a summarizing statement, as he often does, revealing that if his judgment of "the rotten soil" of Jordan County is harsh, he is also well aware of more frightful possibilities: "Here human cruelty was displayed at its worst, you'd say, until you considered the reverse of the medal and saw the possibility of worse cruelty still: an absence of concern, that is, or even curiosity" (148).

The quality of the comedy in *Love in a Dry Season* derives in part from the distancing Foote employs by presenting the situations through the eye of Bristol and interpolating the only less omniscient and slightly more human comments of the narrator. The characters, as Foote claims, create and, therefore, deserve their situations, through which they move virtually unaffected, leaving the reader's sympathies dormant. Drew and the Carruthers couple are stylized almost to the degree of becoming humor-characters, and comedy modulates into farce in the climactic scene of their story.

Drew is a comic creation. He is only superficially like Fitzgerald's Gatsby, with whom he is sometimes compared.[7] True, he comes, like Gatsby, from the "Midwest," takes advantage of opportunities in World War I, and pursues schemes all of which do not bear examination. But Drew has no "Platonic conception" of himself or anything else to make us take him seriously as we do Gatsby. Moreover, nobody in *Love in a Dry Season* or among its readers would pronounce Drew "worth the whole damn bunch put together," as Nick Carraway says of Gatsby, and there is no hint of tragedy in his career. The Carruthers pair resemble the Buchanans in *The Great Gatsby* but only slightly; and, though "the eyes of Doctor T. J. Eckleburg" watch over Fitzgerald's characters as "the great Eye of Bristol" watches those of Shelby Foote, the latter's voyeur theme makes the image appropriate. From the Punch-and-Judy battering to which Drew and the Carruthers pair subject themselves, they bob up triumphantly and, as is the nature of comedy, a balance—albeit of a grimly ironic kind—is restored.

The humor arising from the Drew-Barcroft situation is different from that of the Drew-Carruthers triangle. It is not so sharp and judgmental, and it varies from episode to episode. The difference is a function of the ambivalence in the presentation of Major Barcroft and, therefore, of his daughters. Might he have been otherwise in other times? At any rate, his dignity and independence remain intact even though his delusions and cruelty damn him. He is not trivial as Drew and the Carrutherses are. Certainly sympathy is mixed with the comedy in Foote's depiction of poor dotty Florence, and there is even more sympathy for sincere, dutiful, but limited Amanda.

The management of humor, for example in two key scenes involving Amanda and Drew, is subtle. Drew remains his comic self, and the reader is coolly amused by his desperation when Amanda insists that she is finally ready to elope. But when Drew stuns her with rejection, the smile fades from the reader's lips as he understands Amanda's desolation. Irony mixed with gentleness, sadness, or regret is rare, however, as the dry season advances.

Much of the comic effect results from adroit manipulation of point of view and from Foote's command of language. Although Drew dominates, the limited presentations, now closely held, now removed to the verge of objectivity, are alternated from one character to another; or one character is presented more and then less intimately, each with his own speech. The focus often shifts to the town itself or to the anonymous narrator whose tone accommodates subject and situation. These shifts result in discrepancies, juxtapositions, and repetitions in changed circumstances which, unlike the two scenes in which Drew rejects Amanda, are usually humorous and serve various other purposes, too.[8]

An instance of this technique of Foote's occurs in the episodes in which Drew is shown plotting his application to the Major for Amanda's hand and then in the actual encounter. Drew lies in bed on Sunday morning, listening to church bells while he reviews the plan of his opening campaign. He is distracted into "unwanted memories of his boyhood" and his career to this point and returns with his mind wonderfully concentrated to the "tactics" by which he means to put even memories of Youngstown behind him. He calls at the Barcroft house to "speak to papa." The focus shifts only slightly toward greater objectivity and inclusiveness, remaining on Drew's subjective state yet allowing the Major gradually to dominate. The change of perspective is enough to remind the reader that the Major is who he is and, looking down from the social height of Bristol, in a position to see Harley Drew plain. He contemptuously dismisses his pretension.

The narrator, who speaks in his own voice in a variety of tones, intimately acquainted with the characters and scene yet above and beyond them, is a further source of comic or humorous effect. His intrusions usually add humor although, as we have said, this varies in quality and may shade into other effects. He comments, for example, on the news of Jeff Carruthers's shooting Drew at Briartree following the Major's death in Bristol:

> There was less conjecture here but that was because people believed there was less room, or at any rate occasion, for conjecture. The event, though far less common than in the old days—when, as they said, men were men—was not uncommon; indeed it was fairly cut-and-dried, though not without the tinge of humor that usually accompanies such bloodshed. "Why, yes, of course," they told each other, speaking with the irrefutable positiveness which seems at times to be in direct ratio to the extent of error. For they were wrong. They were utterly and ironically wrong. (198)

Nothing so old-fashioned as a husband's honor, of course, was actually involved. The truth is uglier—and funnier in a cruel way—than Bristol knows; and the narrator reveals it. Drew and Amy had gone brazenly upstairs to bed thinking to gull the blind Jeff while he played recordings of Jelly Roll Morton singing "Two Nineteen" and Bessie Smith singing "Empty Bed." The entire section, entitled "Shots in the Dark," is played out like French bedroom farce of the most exteme heartlessness.

## Chapter Four

# *A Landscape in Narrative*

### The Structure of *Jordan County*

The subtitle of *Jordan County* (1954) is a phrase that may be taken as descriptive of all Shelby Foote's fiction including even *Shiloh,* peripheral to the main body though that is. Calling it *A Landscape in Narrative,* Foote has said that this novel, "if it is a novel . . . has place for its hero and time for its plot. [Jordan County] is the main character in the novel—the land itself. And you go backwards through time to find out what made it what it is."[1] For casual readers, at least, this book must supersede *Tournament* as the key to Foote's work as long as the latter is kept out of print. *Jordan County* provides the most inclusive "plot" since it covers, at least in exposition, time back to the advent of whites. Lacking a protagonist such as Hugh Bart of *Tournament,* it can focus on "the land"; and it contains a more nearly complete account than any of the earlier novels of what made modern Jordan County "what it is."

In raising a question as to whether this book is properly to be called a novel, Foote was referring to the circumstance that it is comprised of seven distinct stories. They are arranged in reverse chronological order, and the reader must infer the articulation. Although written at different times and in some instances previously published in different forms, the stories combine into a whole in somewhat the same ways as those that make up William Faulkner's *Go Down, Moses,* an immediate ancestor, or more remotely, Sherwood Anderson's *Winesburg, Ohio,* and James Joyce's *Dubliners,* among a number of works that have been called "short-story cycles" and that might be mentioned for comparison. The stories are linked to one another and to Foote's other fiction by the setting-through-time. They are further related by the use of his typical themes and recurrent characters and events and by characteristic handling of points of view, distancing, juxtapositions, echoes. Nevertheless, *Jordan County* was a considerable departure from the tight construction and explicit development of previous novels, as if Foote were trying for a new synthesis of his material and searching for a new method.

*Jordan County* is not intended as a complete "historical novel" although it deals with Delta episodes from the mid-twentieth century, the time of the opening story, to the late eighteenth, the time of the last, with a further allusion to the sixteenth. The parts are unevenly developed, some being only sketches, some of novella length; there are discontinuities and a wide range of subjects. If, however, he did not envisage a novel, certainly Foote had in mind subsuming all of the components under the sign of the Delta. He has expressed dissatisfaction with the short story: "It's a form that's unsatisfactory to me unless it's tied in with other things. Then I can get some interest. But to create a perfect little thing doesn't interest me at all. If somehow it were part of a whole—all the short stories I've ever written are tied in; in that book *Jordan County* . . . they are related to each other, and when I get that I'm happy working in the form. But unless I have that, I'm not."[2]

The reader is invited by the arrangement to sense the situation in Bristol, Mississippi, as of about 1950 and then to infer from a sort of social genealogy how matters came to that pass. Since the first piece renders Bristol as a loveless hell, the book will be antiprogress, literally a regression. The stories depict, however, comparatively more human situations at successively earlier epochs; yet the pieces earliest in time concern the advent of the white man and treat his displacement of the Indian as primal sin. By impliction, therefore, the book makes a profoundly pessimistic statement.

A French critic finds in the arrangement of stories an instance of "the interplay of structures" by means of which Foote has worked out an intriguing rapprochement of "the novel" and "history."[3] In this, we surmise that Foote's claim, often repeated, to influence by Proust inheres. Foote himself asserts that he is only searching for understanding, that he is always looking for answers and loses interest if he is "lucky enough to find them."[4] Here, though fragmentary, is a *recherche du temps perdu,* to which fictions both earlier and later may be added as fragments tying in to a larger whole which cannot perhaps ever be completed.

## "Rain Down Home"

*Jordan County* begins with "Rain Down Home," the story of Pauly Green, who following service in World War II returns to his hometown, Bristol, seeking human relationships to sustain him in the precarious balance he has attained after psychiatric treatment. War has not, in this modern instance, made the man. He enters Bristol on the train from Memphis at a blood-colored sunrise and through an intermittently rainy day searches for human contact. Rebuffed repeatedly, Pauly, who has been decorated for marksmanship, returns to a café where he had found only suspiciousness and hostility and shoots up the premises. He ends in the hands of the police. The verdict is "deranged." He is, but so is Bristol.

This story is ambiguous. Foote's constant theme of human loneliness is clearly sounded, but Pauly Green is clinically unstable, his tone abrupt, and his appearance rough. People might have reason to shy away; and, with one exception—Parker Nowell from *Love in a Dry Season,* an especially cold fish as we know—all his encounters are with people he had never known. Although he is returning "home," there is no development of his background beyond the fact that he was once a paper boy and finds Bristol changed for the worse.

To a poor old man who comes to sit in the city park, named for an old family, the Wingates, Pauly recounts his adventures and generalizes about what he knows: "Sad things, terrible things happen to people. . . . Kicked in the teeth, insulted, full of misery the way a glass can get so full it bulges at the brim with surface tension—what does it mean? . . . It's got to mean something, all that suffering." When the old man ventures that "they got away from God," Pauly demands angrily, "Whats God got to do with it? What does He care?" (12).[5]

Pauly goes on to put to the old derelict a question which seems to govern the book in that it haunts the other stories and is more or less explicitly answered in the last two although the connections must be inferred. The old man says that people were never meant to be happy, an idea Pauly rejects. He says, "I want to live in the world but I dont understand, and until I can understand I cant live. Why wont people be happy? Not cant: *wont*" (13).

"Rain Down Home" is presented through a limited omniscient narrator who follows Pauly and comments briefly on the upshot of his return home. The compact story moves quickly through Pauly's meetings with various citizens, each given accurately identifying speech. The weather, especially the rain, gathers symbolic force reminiscent of Hemingway's use of it. The old man has no traditional wisdom to offer the young: life means nothing to him. The traffic lights of Bristol again carry a burden of meaning: "Cars went past or paused at intersections, obedient to the traffic lights suspended between poles, the lidless glare of red and green, the momentary blink of amber, relaying the orders of some central brain, peremptory, electric, and unthinking." Pauly, veteran of the most recent war, "frowned"; later, passing the statue of the Confederate soldier on the courthouse grounds, he looks up and notes "the blank stone eyeballs under the wide-brimmed hat" (5,13).

## "Ride Out"

The second slot in *Jordan County* is allotted to "Ride Out," which is "a perfect little thing" duly justified, according to the author's preference, by integration of Jordan County materials. It deals with the life and death, the latter a direct but triumphant function of the former, of a Negro jazz artist whose music has its impact in the world beyond Jordan County. "Ride Out" is a novella, rewritten from a *Saturday Evening Post* story entitled "Tell Them Good-by" (1947) and a longer "Ride Out" published in *New Short Novels* (1954) which the author describes as "authentic, an intermediate version."[6] Foote explains the title thus: "'Ride out' is a jazz term. When a song has a 'ride out' finish, it means they ride it hard at the end. In the story, the main character, whose name is Duff Conway, dies in the electric chair, and the executioner says he's going to ride him right out of this earth. The term 'ride out' is a jazz term and also applies to the end of his life."[7] Duff Conway is not entirely a victim. He rides out his life as he has his sensational cornet solos.

Complete in itself, Duff Conway's story relates to the other Jordan County fictions in intricate ways. He awaits execution in the same jail cell later occupied by Luther Eustis. The reporter in *Follow Me Down* recalls interviewing Conway there the night before he went to the chair.

The Jeffcoats—the garrulous turnkey and his less sympathetic cousin who operates the "old shocking chair"—figure prominently. The musician is the beloved son of Nora Conway, the Barcrofts' cook in *Love in a Dry Season*, with whom Amanda might have found closer ties through joint experience of grief, but cannot. And Julia Kinship, the sexy, malicious girl in red who precipitates Conway's crime, will later be identified as the sister of Eben Kinship of Memphis, one of the main characters in *September September*.

The time of the story compasses Duff Conway's birth in 1913 and his death in 1940. The first-person narrator is the county physician who attends the execution. During twelve years afterward, he has ferreted out the story from Nora, two older Negro musicians who appreciated and encourged Conway's talent, and an academic New England composer whose musicology and method of composition are changed by his encounter with Conway's "natural genius" during a short period when the latter performs in Harlem. The unnamed physician evidently knows and loves jazz and, honest man that he is, acknowledges his sources, so gaining credibility. He keeps his account objective; but his interest, sympathy, and sense of irony come through the shaping of the story he tells, the carefully rendered details, his attention to speech patterns of others, and his own way of speaking.

The immediate present is the early morning of the day of execution, October 10, 1940, as the officials test the chair and then carry out their duty. The narrator is conscious of Conway's mother and a friend waiting outside the jail in a muledrawn wagon with a pine coffin. The narrator goes back to fill in a narrative that he divides into three carefully shaped parts separated by the delta device ($\Delta$) that becomes a trademark of Foote's longer fiction.

The first part begins with Conway's parents, his mother a fifteen-year-old girl who loves a wandering singer and guitar-player with "a itchy heel." Duff is born on the levee during a flood in an intriguing variation on the motif of the hero who comes by water. He discovers an interest in music, and the narrator traces the mother's concern as music obsesses him. During a sojourn in reform school, the warden gives Duff a dented cornet formerly owned by a youth who died of tuberculosis. It enables him to find an outlet for the music that is his life, but it carries the germs that would have killed him if love, sex, and the law had not proved enough for the purpose.

The second part follows Duff from the Mansion House in Bristol, where he plays with the legendary Blind Bailey, to New Orleans by excursion steamer, performing on the way, to play a new horn with Pearly Jefferson's Basin Six, and in 1935 on to New York where he is tutored by Rex Ingersoll. He is playing in a Harlem club when he attracts the fascinated attention of Harry Van, the New England composer, and then a hemorrhage signals the advance of disease.

In the last section, Conway returns to his mother in Bristol. He cannot rest and try to get well, however, because it means giving up his horn. He sneaks out to play with Blind Bailey, falls in love with Julia Kinship, and allows her to goad him into murdering a rival. Sentenced by Judge Holiman of *Follow Me Down* (unnamed here), he awaits electrocution. The appalled Harry Van comes down to visit him, but the turnkey does most of the talking—not the least service that strange functionary renders his charges. Conway wants nothing but music—which for him means death; and Van leaves with the "clarity and sweetness" of Conway's rendition of "Didn't He Ramble" in his ears.

The culminating relationship is this unusual but plausible friendship between Conway and Van, one of the few instances in Foote's work of human communication across seemingly unbridgeable gulfs. Yale-educated and an advanced student of composition, Van hears Conway at the Black Cat and finds a new world. His aim had been "music that was intellectual in concept and highly organized, with a good deal more stress on form than content." This is the "safest" way, "meaning that it was the one least likely to lead to disappointment; the less you ventured, emotionally, the less you stood to lose." Van begins to write "jazz themes with variations based on Duff's improvisations," then abandons this, knowing "he had got what he wanted by then; he had made the breakthrough, and the influence remained, if not the signs" (44, 48–49).

We suggest that "the influence . . . if not the signs" of jazz is analyzable in Shelby Foote's writing as it is in Harry Van's musical compositions. Composed early and twice revised, "Ride Out" is probably the seminal story in *Jordan County,* and *Jordan County* is accordingly not so "safe" as the earlier books. Essentially what Van learns from Conway is "never let technique be anything but a means to an end" (49). Speaking of jazz, Foote has asserted, ". . . all my life I've heard this music and loved it very much." He distinguishes between good and bad jazz musicians: the good player "was doing his best to communicate with you in an absolutely direct way, loaded with feeling. All his feelings he was putting directly into that music. . . . when he's giving it all he's got, his technique becomes relatively unimportant because there's something about the very basic best of jazz, something about the blues, that communicates from one person to another."[8]

While Duff's relationship with the composer is the intellectual center of the story, his long, painful relationship with his mother is most noteworthy for strength and subtlety. Foote cites it as an example of "what's at the middle of a novel" in explaining why he does not write plays or movie scenarios: "—the boy, the jazz musician in there, is very close to his mother. But they never communicate. His inability to communicate with her is part of the story, and if you do a play in which he communicates with her, you've destroyed the story."[9]

Foote here alludes to a characteristic quality of his work: he writes narrative of such integrity that it resists dramatization. He has, nevertheless, experimented with dramatizing three stories other than "Ride Out" from *Jordan County*. In 1964, his dramatizations of "Rain Down Home," "A Marriage Portion," and "The Freedom Kick" were presented as *Jordan County: A Three-Part Landscape in the Round* by the Arena Stage in Washington.[10]

In the end, Nora, after protesting in every way she knows all his life because she wants him to live, brings the fatal cornet to him in jail. It was dented in the scuffle the night of the murder, and Nora has taken it to a gunsmith to have it repaired. So it is finally music from "the cornet . . . lifted toward the window, catching the light as in a golden bowl," that dominates the conclusion (66). The proposition emerges from the narrative that the incomparable music of Duff Conway is a function of the man's fate and a fulfillment for him.[11]

## "A Marriage Portion"

The third element of *Jordan County* is a four-page dramatic monologue about the mid-1920s introducing again the mordant comedy of *Love in a Dry Season*. Dryly entitled "A Marriage Portion," it is spoken by a bitchy, pampered Bristol woman who chatters about her marriage "back before the flood"—literally before that of 1927, *the* flood in the experience of the Delta. She married one of the emasculated Bristol men for his money—what else would she marry him for? She describes their wedding night at the Robert E. Lee Hotel in Jackson and sums up the bridegroom as "hard on the outside all right, but soggy inside." He drinks too much and is driven, presumably by mixing her with alcohol, to killing flies with a hammer and banging up the silver wedding gifts. After their divorce, he marries twice again. The narrator does not care, "provided that check comes through on the first of every month." In a Browningesque conclusion, it is revealed that she is talking to a current bed-partner: "I guess youd better get up now and go; I think thats daylight peeping through the shade" (74).

The monologue is racy and humorous because of her utter selfishness and her blindness to herself and her situation. Racism shows through when she mentions Negro servants, and about herself she is sentimental and self-pitying. A story of family decline, her father's loss of money and the failure of her parents' marriage, is shadowy in the background. Foote, acknowledging dislike and perhaps fear of "complex" women (though this one is decidedly not complex), has disclaimed any intention of making woman as destroyer a major subject. He added, however, "I agree that woman is a destroyer. If she's allowed to destroy, I think she will."[12] With a father and a husband like those in "A Marriage Portion," the narrator's simple-minded kind of destructiveness is no challenge.

## "Child by Fever"

Foote expanded and deepened his themes of the rapid decline of the first families of Bristol and woman as destroyer in "Child by Fever," a gothic novella of 150 pages which, by virtue of length and position, provides the center of gravity in *Jordan County*. It is "at the middle of the novel" and has at its own middle a mother-son relationship of the planter class paralleling that between Nora Conway and Duff in "Ride Out." The work exists in two other versions, a story of thirty pages published in *New World Writing: Fourth Mentor Selection* (1953) and a "third draft" from 1950 in the Percy Library in Greenville.[13]

It is the story of Hector Wingate Sturgis, set within the history of the Wingate family before and after the life span of the central figure. The omniscient narrator, like the one in *Love in a Dry Season,* knows Bristol but is also above and beyond it. He comments, "There were only three main dates to hang it [Hector's story] on—1878, 1899, 1911: the years of his birth, his marriage, and his death—which is as much as most men have, and more than some" (77). The reader will recall this statement when Hector hangs himself; the delayed implication seems to be that the dates of his birth and marriage might have been as appropriate for his purpose as the one he finally chose.

The narrator has explained that Hector's mother, Esther Wingate Sturgis, is remembered long after Hector's tale is told because Bristol's new residential sections were carved from the Wingate plantation and because she gave the city the land for Wingate Park, where Pauly Green was to have dispiriting encounters. The Wingate family has been in the Delta since 1835. Its history is kept dimly alive in periodic newspaper stories and pictures of Mrs. Sturgis, who becomes "the old lady in the wheelchair, her eyes like agates set into the sockets of a skull, and the caption always calls her the mother of Bristol" (224).

The title alludes to yellow fever, which periodically ravaged the Delta and was raging the year Hector was born. Later, his father and his Grandmother Wingate die of fever while he is away at school. Decades afterward, Bristol believes that Mrs. Sturgis will never die because she was "baked to durability in the oven of the fever" (76).

The effect on the unborn Hector may be suggested by Foote's explanation that his title also alludes to "William James's Varieties of Religious Experience (p 15) [sic]: 'For aught we know to the contrary, 103° or 104° Fahrenheit might be a much more favorable temperature for truths to germinate and sprout in, than the more ordinary blood-heat of 97 or 98 degrees.' This seemed to me to tie in with the morbidity of that work ["Child by Fever"], an attempt to write a modern gothic novella. It was also a second attempt ('Ride Out' was the first) to deal with the juxtaposition of the artist against the backdrop of Society. Youll notice they both lost."[14]

The novella is divided into three long chapters, each having three distinct divisions. These are marked by the delta sign. The narrator begins and ends with the mother, who dies, nearing ninety, about 1950. The story comes full circle, ending shortly after her death.

Her story in turn is set against a backdrop of family history revealed from present to past. Her father, the second Hector, is a soured planter who, somewhat like Major Barcroft, resents having missed the chance for "a swirl of glory" in the Civil War. He remained at home under the Twenty-Negro clause of the Conscription Act, while his three brothers fought; and he "felt that he had failed his heritage." He cannot attend the gatherings of the veterans and comes to resent both his wife, daughter of a rich levee contractor, and his only child. The wife, Esther Wingate, is a strong-willed woman who turns her smothering attention to the daughter, named Esther also. The second Hector is killed, in a disagreement over a crop settlement in 1877, by a Negro tenant, who is lynched on Christmas morning. "Thus at last he achieved his heritage of violence; it had been a bloody death, if not a hero's" the narrator comments (79, 84). Soon—much too soon—after her father's death, the second Esther Wingate, joined in unending combat with her mother, becomes pregnant out of spite and has to marry the son of an Irish barkeeper. John Sturgis is an enterprising salesman for a feed and grain company, but the unequal marriage creates a scandal which is not lessened when the baby arrives too soon.

The first Hector Wingate had achieved death by violence in a heroic way. After making a fortune in the newly opened Delta and building the big, fine Wingate house, he had died in Mexico fighting under Jefferson Davis at Buena Vista. Ruin begins, then, in the second generation, and we have another instance of Foote's Delta families in which ruin of the women is traced to weakness and decline in their men. Old Samuel, whose life with the Wingates has taken him from stable boy and coachman to superannuated cast-off living in a Wingate shack, makes a speech about diminishing manhood. Looking back to the first Hector, he observes: "Yassah, and he was a proud, tall man in his day. . . . I members the morning he rode off to war, the one before the big one, and never come back. . . . It appear to me lak everything is shrunk, and me along with um. Even the watermillions is little bitty" (214).

The third Hector is doomed "to fail his heritage" from the moment he is conceived on the front seat of a buggy after choir practice. His father is despised by Mrs. Wingate and emasculated by his bitter mother. After his father's death, Hector cannot remember his face. Hector, born into scandal and gossip about "the highborn," inevitably creates enough of his own to last the town until the Barcroft-Drew-Carruthers scandal supersedes it some thirty years later. Dominated by his formidable grandmother, who despotically rules the plantation, he makes as a child one feeble attempt to gain self-respect by violence. Encouraged by the coachman who drives him to school, he attacks with his fine book satchel a group of boys who follow the coach to taunt the school sissy. But he cannot persevere and becomes nauseated.

Withdrawn from school to be tutored at home, he is later sent to a Virginia boarding school and returns to find his grandmother and father dead and his mother firmly ensconced in his grandmother's place, like her even in looks. Again he makes an attempt to become a person in his own right, and again he fails. Upon graduation from the University of Virginia, he starts to enlist in the company of volunteers commanded by Major Barcroft in 1898, but his mother forbids. Under her harsh tutelage, he tries to become a planter but fails.

Hector, "a dude" in a "bright-spoked surrey," lives the social life of Bristol until in a gesture of independence he, too, marries beneath his class, not for spite but for love. Daughter of a misshapen seamstress, Ella Lowry has a reputation for promiscuity but has on her own volition become a "Magdalen redeemed." She and Hector are related through his Irish grandfather, and she tells him of a "heritage of violence" on this side too. The old grandfather murdered his wife and her lover with an axe and fled for America. Hector thinks of "the stain of blood carried down from father to son and from father to son" (143).

Continuing in love with his wife, Hector fails as a husband. Their child is born at home, and the difficulty of the birth so affects Hector that he becomes impotent. The baby is defective and soon dies. Then Ella turns promiscuous again, and Hector, after an attempt to control her which she welcomes but he cannot carry through, dissolves in tears. In a repetition of the story of his Grandfather Sturgis's deed, he buys a sharp axe to kill her with but of course cannot use it. The climax comes when she is discovered dead of accidental asphyxiation with her drummer lover in the local hotel. Hector, an increasingly deranged recluse, begins to imagine that she comes from her grave to his room to talk with him.

Hector finds one outlet that absorbs him and provides some consolation in his years of heartbreak and isolation. Gifted at mechanical drawing, he produces plans for the subdivisions successively built on the plantation acres. His drawings become more detailed and fanciful as the years pass. After his death, his mother gives them, handsomely bound, to the city "as the Wingate bid for a place in the world of art." They remain on display in the city hall for twenty years. The townspeople see "the crowded, multicolored sheets that had begun as maps and wound up resembling work done by a latter-day amateur Bruegel or Bosch looking down from a seat in the clouds" as evidence that Hector Sturgis "was crazy as a betsy bug" (144, 147). The planter manqué becomes the artist manqué, and bits and pieces of his lurid story are all that remain.

Foote often presents his "modern gothic" elements in an ironic light that gives freshness to the conventions. Against the background of family hatred among the Wingates there is camouflaged hatred between the races. Little Hector's Negro nurse regales him with stories of demons, Dobby Hicks the guardian angel, and "raw head and bloody bones." She has a store of charms or "mojoes," and she further distresses the child by laughing wickedly from her pallet beside Hector's bed as she hears his mother berating his father in the next room. In old age, her "second sight" enables her to see some unnamed and terrifying evil in Hector when, in a rare outgoing gesture, he stops to see her while he is on a walk. She thinks he is Satan, and he who had always run from things flees from her cabin as he has never fled before.

Adding to the gothic effect is the hidden story of old Sturgis's past, hidden relationships, and the bizarre story of Ella's death. Hector has a monstrous mother-in-law as well as monstrous offspring. The story of the fever and its consequences, into which Foote slips the "shape-shifter" motif when Mrs. Sturgis replaces Mrs. Wingate, increases the strangeness and horror. The little boy discovers the attic in the Wingate house while the household naps. He lives a secret life there among "the conglomerate litter," including the Confederate uniforms of his dead great-uncles that "dangled side by side like hanged men" (104). Here he hangs himself but has an aborted flash of recognition as too late he hears laughter and tries to say, "This is wrong." In the stifling August heat, he is soon discovered.

The narrator works all these elements into an account that is rich in glimpses of Bristol life and history. Some of his best description comes in his presentation of the "dominants" of the place—"the trees, the war, the Negroes, the river . . ." (108–9). Taken altogether, the novella conveys the idea that even in "the visitable past," in James's words, an hereditary curse hangs over Hector Sturgis. The haunting of the madman is the most horrible event. Ella comes repeatedly, decaying from visit to visit, to the closed room from which Hector ceases to emerge; he follows her with childlike faith to his childhood domain in the attic.

## "The Freedom Kick"

By its brevity and position "The Freedom Kick" invites comparison with "A Marriage Portion." Foote also builds on a marked contrast: the latter features a despicable modern white woman, the other a black woman who risks all for freedom in Reconstruction times. Only a sketch, "The Freedom Kick" echoes elements in other stories. It is about the daughter of a freedman in slavery time, of "blood pride" and a child who disappoints the parent by forced marriage to "the artist type," here a Negro photographer. But the woman in question keeps "the blood pride," and her son, the narrator, has it, too.

The action centers in hideous, heartless violence in which black is cruel to black as well as white to black and each other. The story only hints at Reconstruction as a historical trauma in Bristol. Its theme is the love of freedom at any cost; the irony lies in the suggestion that for the blacks it was illusory.

## "Pillar of Fire"

The phrase "pillar of fire" associated with Southern houses burning by night, especially during the Civil War, has haunted Shelby Foote's imagination. From Jackson to Vicksburg, the region he grew up in was full of the reminders. Some remain, ruined chimneys marking the spots where in 1863 Sherman, in cooperation with Grant, rehearsed for his more famous march to the sea through Georgia, and where in the last years of the war other houses were burned in reprisal for partisan activity. There were also such remains from other times, wooden houses in rural sections being always in jeopardy.

In *Tournament,* Hugh Bart's father, who, like Foote's great-grandfather, lived in the Black Prairie section, thinks that "his house or his barn might be the next to go up in a pillar of fire" because he refuses to join the Ku Klux Klan during Reconstruction (70). Luther Eustis in *Follow Me Down* remembers standing with his grandfather "on a road that began on a night over forty years ago" watching his home go up in a fire his father had set: "When the roof caved in, the sparks made a tall round tower, a pillar of fire roaring up and up. . . ." His wife Kate also describes this burning: ". . . there was a pillar of fire going straight up into the night, so bright the stars were pale" (89, 203).

Foote chose the phrase for the title of the story which remains, pending further elaboration of his Jordan County material, central in his work. The title, recalling only accidentally the biblical pillar of fire, alludes to the burning by Union soldiers of the original house on Solitaire, the home of Foote's grand old man, Isaac Jameson. Enlarged, remodeled, and enlarged again from the three-room structure Isaac and his slaves erected in 1820, it becomes a mansion, fine, but not nearly so fine as the one built for Clive Jameson. The latter is a house of three stories and forty rooms built by a New Orleans architect (but modeled by Shelby Foote on his grandfather's Mt. Holly) for Isaac's son, General Clive Jameson, from whom Hugh Bart acquires it (in *Tournament*).

Isaac Jameson's founding of Solitaire, which is central in "Pillar of Fire," is also briefly presented in *Tournament*. Comparison of the 1949 passage with the finished story of 1954 leads to insight into the continuous and interlocking nature of Foote's Delta materials and appreciation of his increasing power and skills.[15] We shall not be surprised to find that Solitaire and the burning of Isaac Jameson's house figure either in a third rendition or at least symbolically in Foote's work in progress.

"Pillar of Fire" is composed as a story within a story. A French commentator speaks of its circularity or coiling structure.[16] The long, three-part narrative of Isaac's life—his origins and young manhood, his middle years, his old age and last thoughts—is framed by a first-person account of the burning of the house and death of Isaac. The seemingly unlikely narrator is Lieutenant Lundy, chosen to accompany his colonel and thirty Negro infantrymen from the Union gunboat *Starlight* on the Mississippi on a burning expedition in reprisal for sniping from the levee. The time is October 1864. Vicksburg has fallen, and Lincoln has announced that the Mississippi now "flows unvexed to the sea." There are still certain "vexations" along the banks, however. Colonel "One-Eye" Frisbie, Lundy's superior, takes vindictive pleasure in making the Southerners "pay" for the eye he lost at Shiloh and the shame he feels for briefly having joined the skulkers under the bluff before emerging to fight again. This fierce New Englander, an abolitionist and worker for the underground railroad, is in distinct contrast to the narrator.

Lundy, a more relaxed Yankee, has a ruined knee from Chancellorsville. Old Isaac sees him as hard-faced and compares him to his son Clive, whose face had also hardened in fires of a war that had lasted too long. Nevertheless, Lundy reveals himself to be sane, perceptive, and sympathetic. He has fought bravely and learned to tell himself "that the bullets flew both ways" and "it was primarily a question of whose home was being invaded" (235). He begins with a description of the march to Solitaire through "land . . . desolated as if by plague," provides Frisbie's background and his own, and breaks off when at noon he enters the ominously silent house. He finds an ancient man, who cannot speak plainly, by the cold hearth, guarded by a tall old Negro whose jaws, one badly swollen, are bound up by a linen dinner napkin.

After Isaac Jameson's part, Lundy closes the framework. His monologue resumes at sunset as he rides beside Frisbie while their sweating men march through heavy dust on the return to the gunboat. They stop for ten minutes, allowing Lundy to look back, see the flames of Solitaire, and relive the events of the afternoon. He is profoundly troubled. He tries to be charitable, but his dislike of his colonel is clear. Frisbie, uneasy because of Lundy's abstracted manner, demands whether or not the lieutenant likes him. Lundy gives an answer that can be interpreted in multiple ways: "Yes, sir, . . . I have come to feel very close to you through these past fourteen months" (279).

During the afternoon, Lundy, under Frisbie's vengeful orders, had supervised the evacuation of the house. Three elderly Negroes, one deaf, one lame, one half-witted, live with the old master. Under the anxious care of the deaf serving man, Isaac Jameson is carried out in his tall armchair to the lawn to watch the burning. The lame cook goes, too, but Lundy has to go back into the burning house to bring down the half-witted woman, who had hidden upstairs. As the heat 'becomes intense, Isaac Jameson struggles to speak and suffers a final stroke. Lundy sees in his "dead eyes a stereoscopic reflection of the burning house repeated in double miniature." The half-witted woman furiously questions the Yankees' claim to be soldiers, saying, "Burners is all you is. Aint you hurt him enough aready? Shame on you!" Later, looking back across wilderness and lake as the house collapses, Lundy sees "a tall column of fire that stood upright for a long minute. . . . " He tries to recall verses from Job: *"Yet man is born unto trouble, as the sparks fly upward. . . . "* But he can remember only the words of the woman (279, 280–81).

For the three balanced, symmetrical sections focused on Isaac Jameson, Foote shades into ominiscient narration to tell Isaac's life and the history of Solitaire. Description and exposition are blended with action, "picture" with "scene." Lyrical touches reveal that the author's imagination is profoundly involved, and symbolism of fire and sun is pervasive.[17] Taken alone, Lundy's framing monologues make a stirring tale. But they truly frame the story of Isaac and Solitaire, providing focus and perspective. "Pillar of Fire," with its links to Foote's previous fiction and work to come, its working in of multiple themes foreshadowed and developed in other texts, commands the central position in the canon.

In his later years, Isaac claimed that he was "a log cabin boy" but in fact was the son of a wealthy Carolina merchant loyal to the Crown who moved to Natchez during the Revolution and reestablished himself. Isaac was born in a wilderness shack on the trek west. He proves wild and will not settle as his brothers do into the family pattern. His father explains him as "wilderness born, conceived in a time of revolution"; he has in his blood "some goading spark of rebellion, some fierce, hot distillate of the jungle itself" (240). After ten adventurous years, he takes a settlement from his family and goes into the "northern wilderness" with trappers in 1818, camps by Lake Jordan, and has a remarkable dream.

Isaac's dream, "repeated three times with a mystical clarity," is taken from *Tournament* (32–33). Set in an expanded context and subtly revised, in "Pillar of Fire" it becomes a prophecy. Under the open sky, "surrounded by lake-country beauty," Isaac dreams of "an army of blacks marching upon the jungle," clearing and plowing fields; ". . . and now the fields began to be striped with the pale green lines of plants soon burdened with squares, then purple-and-white dotted, then deep red with blooms, then shimmering white in the summer heat." He dreams the cycle of the Delta year: the cotton is picked, the fields become "brown and desolate in the rain," and the stalks go "down into bottomless mud. Then in the the dream there was quiet, autumnal death until the spring returned and the plowmen . . ." (243–44).

He makes the dream come true. Claiming 1,800 acres to begin with, by 1826 he has 3,200. At fifty, having named the plantation Solitaire to confirm "his bachelor intentions," he marries for love a twenty-year-old girl with beautiful arms and hair who sometimes works in the taproom of her father's inn in the village of Ithaca by the lake. It is a good marriage. Kate is the undisputed mistress of the house, which she aspires to make the finest in the area. Isaac is the prosperous planter, youthful-looking, impressive, dignified.

Isaac comes to think of his life as divided into three phases. The first included "fifty years spent running hard after trouble in any form." The second phase, the good years after he marries, lasts until he is nearly eighty. These are good years for Jordan County as well—or so they seem. By the 1850s, cotton is becoming king, the small farmers around Lake Jordan move north, and "their claims were gobbled up by those who stayed, as well as by others who moved in on their heels." This "second wave of comers" is described as alien to Isaac and the other founders. They "were essentially businessmen . . . [who] could juggle figures and balance books and put the profits where they earned more profits" (248, 251).

The culture remained thin and was vulgarized. With few exceptions, nobody read; everybody was interested in translating cotton into money. The new nabobs of Lake Jordan built mansions in imitation of those in tidewater Virginia but could not make up for their lack of breeding. "Their pleasures were few and simple and usually violent, limited mainly to hunting and poker." A favorite Sunday afternoon amusement was to watch the Negro Memzy butt heads with a bull in the Jameson barnlot. But the planters had the arrogance of their pretensions: "Insecurity had bred a semblance of security, until now no one questioned their right to anything at all" (252, 257–58).

Isaac has a son, Clive, born in 1833, "the year the stars fell"—he is given the sobriquet "the Starborn Brigadier" during the Civil War. Isaac educates him at the Virginia Military Institute, where T. J. Jackson teaches him mathematics; but his education does not matter if only he does not become infected by books. For he is destined for a planter, educated in "the particular temper and whims of cotton as well as the temper and whims of the people who worked it, meaning Negroes" (253). When Clive marries, Isaac and Katy build the splendid second mansion at Solitaire as their wedding present. In the meanwhile, Isaac is troubled during the 1850s as talk of disunion develops. Like Andrew Jackson, under whom he fought in 1812, he believes in Union. He has seen enough fighting in his time, but he gives up urging sanity.

Even before Sumter, Clive Jameson joins an elite cavalry troop and goes away, to return when it disbands and then go to war in earnest. By the middle of the war, he is a glittering hero, changed, hardened. Most of the slaves are gone from Solitaire, the new house is closed, Clive's wife and sons are on the Gulf Coast, and the upper floor of the old house is sealed off. At fifty-six Katy dies.

Isaac Jameson at the age of eighty-six is well into his last narrow, confined phase. Only three Negroes remain, and food is scarce. The quarters are burned by soldiers from a Union platoon when the half-witted Negress protests their tearing up cabins for firewood by revealing that they belong to the famous General Jameson. This act presages the later burning of Isaac's house.

The morning after this first fire, Isaac has a stroke. Unable to speak plainly, he wanders, often to a section of Solitaire where he had seen a deserted Choctaw village on his first trip into the wilderness. The rosy-colored bricks for Clive's house had come from a clay deposit near the village.

The place draws Isaac, who, though he "had never been one for abstract thinking," ponders certain questions and applies what he remembers to himself. The Indians "were gone now, casualties not of war but of progress, obsolete. . . . He and his kind, the pioneers, the land-grabbing hungry rough-shod men who had, like the flatboat river bullies before them, that curious combination of bravado and deadly earnestness, loving a fight for the sake of the fight itself and not the outcome—were they to disappear, having served their purpose, and leave no more trace than the Choctaws?" He questions "the dignity of man," remembers the clearing of the land and his prosperity, and concludes, "the earth endures." And he comes to what has been foreshadowed as the central symbolism of the story when he thinks, "It all goes back to fire!" (269, 270).

Giving up his walks, Isaac grows more emaciated and his speech deteriorates further. Still trying to fathom his "abstractions," he ponders God's judgment—though he has not been a believer—and comes again to this: "It's the sun and we go back there, back to fire" (270). In the heat of late October, Colonel Frisbie sends Lundy in.

Into Isaac Jameson's reflections following his first stroke, Shelby Foote has worked phrasing which will remind the attentive reader of Pauly Green's question in the opening story of *Jordan County*: why *won't* people be happy? We read that Isaac Jameson, the strong founder, no less than Pauly, the alienated posterity, "groped for an answer." Knowing nothing about aphasia, Isaac thinks "maybe God had touched him" since he finds himself speaking in tongues like people at frontier revivals. "But if it was God it was punishment, since it had not come through faith. He must be under judgment, just as maybe the whole nation was, having to suffer for the double sin of slavery and mistreatment of the land" (270). Ultimately, as noted, he returns to his stark formula to the effect that all goes back to fire; but he has touched, in a way more significant for the reader than the character himself, on the theme of mistreatment of the land, predicated upon abuse of people—Indians, Negro slaves, anybody who got in the way of cotton and money—as proximate causes of the Delta's predicament.

## "The Sacred Mound"

"The Sacred Mound," included in a 1979 anthology of Southern literature to represent Shelby Foote, [18] is presented as a translation of a Spanish legal document concerning a criminal case. It is the "Declaration" and "Disposition" of the case of a Choctaw, Chisahahoma, known also as John Postoak, so that the reader speculates about his relationship to Isaac Jameson's slave with the toothache in "Pillar of Fire" whose name is Postoak. Recorded in ornate official Spanish by a scrivener, the document is addressed to his superior by the Provisional Governor of Mississippi, his name and titles translated literally as "Mr John the Baptist of Elquezable, Lieutentant Colonel of Cavalry and Provisional Governor of this said Province of Mississippi." Dated 23 September 1797, from "the town of Natchez and garrison of St Iago"—it is the year before the Spanish evacuated and left the area to the Americans—the document concerns "the grisly murders" of two Americans by the Choctaws. This description of the event is that of the Spanish official. For their part, the Choctaws regarded it as the execution of a sentence after due tribal consideration and ceremony (283–84).

When the tribe is stricken by an epidemic of smallpox contracted from one of the white men, the great chief sends Chisahahoma, "a singer" and descendant of "singers" (and so the earliest in time of the artist types in Foote's fiction), to make amends to the white man's god, sacrifice himself, and so remove the curse. Chisahahoma does sacrifice himself but in a way not intended. Kindly treated by the priest of a Natchez church, he is taught and converted and goes of his own accord to the Spanish authorities. Seeking to act upon the principles of his newly acquired Christian faith, he confesses the homicides as his own.

Having heard the story of the deaths of the two Americans and all that led up to them, Mr John the Baptist of Elquezable recommends, in a gesture of ironic contempt, that the Indian be freed. For he "has renounced his former worship which led him to participate in these atrocities"; the priest has given assurance that Postoak will become "a missionary among his heathen people"; and in any case the Spanish are "preparing to depart this barbarous land" and leave it "to them of the North." Furthermore, "the victims were neither of our Nation nor our Faith" (298). As to whether or not Chisahahoma actually removed "the curse" on his people, all of Shelby Foote's work implies a clear answer: No. The particular curse of smallpox came from the white man; it may pass, but the white man himself, fertile source of curses, will remain. Is not the virus of Christianity now to be transmitted by Chisahahoma?

Asked whether or not the story is really a translation, Foote answered that it is and did not elaborate. Common sense and study of Foote's fiction lead to the conclusion that the skeleton of the document was given improved articulation, flesh, and life by the author. His characteristically careful shaping, the building to a crucial point of interest before divisions, the subtle characterization and use of language, the descriptive passages and working in of historical detail, and the irony all indicate that "the singer" here is Shelby Foote. The Spanish governor's tone, proud and chauvinistic, is conveyed in his dictation. Much of the document being in the form of questions and answers by the prisoner, there was opportunity to convey the distinctive phrasing of the Indian governed by tribal experience and custom.

Incidentally to his account of the killing of the two Americans, Chisahahoma reviews the history of the relationships between his people and white men. He starts with the coming of "the man Soto," whereupon the scandalized governor interposes, "so he called him, of glorious memory in the annals of Spain: Hernando de Soto." But in the annals of the Choctaws, the burial of the man Soto in the Mississippi had desecrated the great river. The governor is not disturbed by the Indian's recital of the legend of his people according to which "the Spaniards . . . wore blisters on their palms with excess of killing— swinging their swords and lances wearily and standing in blood to the rowels of their spurs. . . ." They disappear, the only proof of their advent the "rusting bits of armor and the horse skulls raised on poles in the long-house yard." Missionaries come and go; the Choctaws keep their gods. Other whites come, always by the river, to gather furs, especially beaver, "a creature not even a boy would hunt," and they cause trouble about women (284, 285–86).

Chisahahoma's discourse deepens to pathos and sharpens to irony when he tries to work in his recently accepted Christian beliefs— neither the pathos nor the irony being conscious on his part, of course. In these passages, Foote seems to us to have formulated, although he has

not as yet amplified and developed anywhere in his fiction, the fundamental theme not only of *Jordan County* but of his still growing vision of
his material as a whole. It appears that the killing of the two Americans,
who were trappers, was the result of warnings against the perfidy of
white men brought to Chisahahoma's tribe by ambassadors from tribes
from farther south.

Their own people having been ruined through trusting whites who
called them "Brother," the ambassadors warn what will happen if
Chisahahoma's people have anything to do with whites. First, the white
men boast of their gods and seek a certain yellow metal. Then they may
be expected to exchange, in guile, "valuables for the worthless pelts of
animals" and pretend to live peaceably with the Indians. But they will
only be leading up to an atrocious proposal (286).

The ambassadors report that the white men "began to ask a strange
thing of us, seeking to buy the land. Sell us the land, they said: Sell us
the land. And we told them, disguising our horror: No man owns the
land; take and live on it; it is lent you for your lifetime; are we not
brothers?" The word "brothers" takes on additional irony through the
Christian interpretation Chisahahoma puts upon it. The white men
settled in, built their houses and towns, brought in their women and
multiplied, and imposed their laws with "the whip and the branding
iron and often the rope." It was not long before the white men drove the
Indians out altogether (287).

Here, then, seems to be the answer for which Isaac Jameson gropes:
the white man, whether French, Spanish, or Anglo, defined as a curse
upon the land because he insists on owning and exploiting and consum-
ing it regardless of the claims of human brotherhood. Isaac was rendered only momentarily uneasy by his memories of the expulsion of the
Choctaws from their village and the land that became part of
Solitaire—and so the name resonates again. It was bought at the price of
human solidarity. Only momentarily, he speculates whether the Civil
War was a judgment not only upon him but upon the whole United
States, a judgment in the form of fratricidal war. *Jordan County* comes to
an acknowledgment of a specific primal sin, the wages of which will be
collected by the latest generation, such as poor Pauly Green in "Rain
Down Home."

# Chapter Five
# A Historical Novel

In Shelby Foote's short novel, *Shiloh,* a reflective character involved in the battle expresses the opinion that books about war are typically written to be read by God Almighty. The reason is that authors arrogate to themselves views of the whole, and "no one but God ever saw it that way." He goes on to say, "A book about war, to be read by men, ought to tell what each . . . of us saw in our own little corner. Then it would be the way it was—not to God but to us." Hearing this, another character gets the point but thinks, "Nobody would do it that way. It would be too jumbled. People when they read, and people when they write, want to be looking out of that big Eye in the sky, playing God" (164).[1] But Foote did it that way in *Shiloh,* and the result is anything but jumbled. In fact, he comes close to having it both ways. He creates artfully assorted and deployed individual points of view, each seeing its own little corner, from which the reader infers without any sense of authorial manipulation what the whole must have been like.

In addition to invented characters through whose points of view the material is shaped and presented, the novel contains historical persons. These "speak the words they spoke and do the things they did at Shiloh," the author declares in a note. Many incidents actually occurred "even when here they are assigned to fictional persons," Foote adds; and he hopes "the weather is accurate too." He canvassed the site of the battle, preserved as a national park, in order to gain direct impressions, which he supplemented by study of Mathew Brady's photographs. In his note, he cites the official reports and secondary sources on which he chiefly relied, ranging from contemporary to modern accounts (225–26). Accepting the scholarship as unexceptionable, one asks of *Shiloh* novelistic values transcending the scholarship.

The fictional characters are conceived realistically in the main but not entirely so since they are personifications of various experiences of the battle. Taken severally, they do not affect the reader as types, but they acquire a stylized quality as he proceeds from one to another. Each speaks a monologue, and what the reader carries away from the novel is a cumulative effect of the different responses to the same situation. Here, as in *Follow Me Down,* Browning's *The Ring and the Book* has been acknowledged as an influence by Foote.

*Shiloh* is composed of seven monologues by six characters, one of whom speaks twice, at the beginning and end, to frame the narrative. Another is a bravura composite, a squad whose members speak individually but together convey the "strange" circumstance "that the twelve of us had been brought together by an event which separated brothers and divided the nation" (163). War may be a sum of individual experiences, but one of those is the experience of a kind of community, forced but real.

The characters are alternately Confederate and Union, beginning and ending, however, with a Southerner. The result is that the balanced presentation tips at last to the South in the sense that the last word is spoken from the Southern point of view. There is nothing chauvinistic in Foote's so disposing the last word. He is suggesting that the battle would haunt the loser, who was doomed to retrospective analysis and rationalization. The victor could put the battle behind him and go on to the future and fresh concerns. The characters vary in age, rank, and background. They see action in various parts of the field on both sides of the line of battle, so that the reader acquires, piece by piece, a mosaic of the entire engagement.

The novel is bathed in poignancy deriving from the tone of Lieutenant Palmer Metcalfe, who speaks at the beginning and at the end. His character and fate, while realistically rendered, discreetly symbolize those of the Confederacy at its most romantic. He is nineteen, the scion of an aristocratic New Orleans family whose connections put him in a position to know the Confederate generals and to have access to Southern strategy. His name and rank, followed by designation as aide-de-camp on the staff of the Southern commander, Albert Sidney Johnston, head the first chapter.

There we see him in his elegantly tailored uniform with fire-gilt buttons and red silk scarf riding a fine horse to the field, where he will help put finishing touches to General Beauregard's battle order. The seventh and final chapter, in which we see him bedraggled during the retreat after the defeat of the Southern forces, is headed plainly: "Palmer Metcalfe, Unattached." He has been unhorsed and must limp in his boots, made by Jeanpris Brothers in New Orleans "strictly for riding." Surrounded by men wounded, dying, and dead as a result of the miscarriage of the battle order whose literary style he had polished, he finds himself pelted by an unseasonable storm. "My boots made a crunching sound in the sleet," he recalls at the end (222).

The character Palmer Metcalfe functions two ways. Foote develops him as an individual but also, by virtue of his social position, uses him structurally as the nearest approach in the narrative to "that big Eye in the sky." The two functions interact. At the beginning, Metcalfe is naively inclined to arrogate to himself some capacity for divine perspective but is brought to a more chastened attitude. Still, he is a study only in definition and redefinition of Southern romanticism, one point implied by the novel being that Southern romanticism was not corrected. Disillusionment, irony, and melancholy have been accommodated only to enrich and darken the romantic mind.

For Metcalfe is a witness to Nathan Bedford Forrest's exploits in the episode at the Fallen Timbers. The very name is a romantic euphemism for the chaotic scene of an abandoned lumbering operation where Forrest attempted an audacious rear-guard action. Charging headlong, he found himself fifty yards in front of his men, isolated among Union infantry. When he realized the situation, Forrest wheeled his horse to escape, received a bullet, but lifting a Union soldier as a shield made his get-away. At this juncture, Metcalfe, thrown from his horse and his breath knocked out, looked up from the ground and "saw something that made me forget that breathing had anything to do with living": Forrest high on his horse and his saber flashing. As Southern hero on the Homeric scale, Forrest becomes an ideal to which Metcalfe can commit himself despite the bloody realities (213).

Not two years earlier, Metcalfe was a cadet at the Louisiana State Military Academy under the command of Tecumseh Sherman. Foote represents the boy as overhearing a conversation between Sherman and one of the professors as they discussed the news of South Carolina's secession. Sherman, who was to be derided even in the North as insane when, after the war began, he declared it a much more serious proposition than anybody imagined, analyzed the illusions of the South in thinking it could win a modern industrial war against the North. In the aftermath of Shiloh, where Sherman's views were vindicated and Grant began to emerge as the ungentlemanly but effectual general the North required, Metcalfe had to do his "spilt-milk thinking."

As the battle began, he fantasized himself capturing Sherman and reminding him of his prediction that the South was bound to fail because it was "totally unprepared, with a bad cause to start with." In defeat, Metcalfe "was through with visions of facing Sherman in his tent and forcing him at pistol point to admit that he was wrong." But in the charge at the Fallen Timbers he nevertheless "found the answer, the oversight in his [Sherman's] argument. He hadnt mentioned Forrest or men like Forrest, men who did not fight as if odds made the winner, who did not necessarily believe that God was on the side of the big battalions, who would charge a brigade with half a regiment of weary men and send that brigade stumbling back to its tents demoralized and glad to be let alone." Trudging away from Shiloh, Metcalfe "determined that when I got back to Corinth I would get myself another horse and enlist under Forrest, commissioned or not" (217, 219, 218–19).

Metcalfe's association at his academy with Sherman is a good example of Foote's use of a fictional character as vehicle for conveying historical data without allowing the account to degenerate from fiction to exposition. As an upper-class young Southerner, Metcalfe could also be persuasively represented as having met or heard knowledgeable talk about the Confederate leaders. In particular, he had through his father a connection with Albert Sidney Johnston. As an aide on Johnston's staff, he is in a position to know the facts of the Confederate situation. He is assigned, as we have mentioned, to assist in the preparation of the Shiloh order according to Beauregard's plan. This was, in fact, based on Napoleon's Waterloo order, Beauregard having his Napoleonic aspirations, but Foote phases into fiction by having Metcalfe help write it. The boy excitedly watches it grow from "notes and discussion" about a "complicated" and problematical situation until it is completed and seems to him "so good, so beautifully simple, it made me catch my breath" (13).

Foote uses Metcalfe's naive participation in planning the engagement to novelistic effect by giving him a premonition: it occurs to him while working on the order "that all battle orders . . . would all result in victory if they were followed." The suspensefulness of the narrative, which deals after all with events of which we know the outcome before we begin to read, derives mainly from Metcalfe's rapid and violent experience of finding that what "worked so well on paper—the flat, clean paper" did not "work out that way on the ground, which was neither flat nor clean—nor, as it turned out, dry" (13, 14). As the various characters are plunged into what proves to be bloody chaos, the reader, like Metcalfe, has the battle plan in the back of his mind and feels the suspense as events rewrite the order.

Although he uses Metcalfe to convey a great deal of information, Foote also develops him steadily as a character. The Napoleonic battle order makes the boy catch his breath at the beginning of the novel. At the end, following traumatic experience of actual battle, the breath is knocked out of him. Looking up from that ground neither flat nor clean or dry, to which he has been thrown, he sees Forrest in mythic perspective and does not need breath. He is Metcalfe still, reacting to events as his nature and breeding dictate, and history has been melded with fiction.

The characters from the Union side who speak in *Shiloh* are Captain Walter Fountain, adjutant of the 53d Ohio regiment; Private Otto Flickner, a cannoneer with the 1st Minnesota Battery; and a squad with an Indiana regiment. The arrangement of these monologues, interspersed with those of the Confederate characters without bridging sections, is essential to the form of the novel. Besides Lieutenant Metcalfe, the Southern characters are Private Luther Dade, a rifleman with the 6th Mississippi, and Sergeant Jefferson Polly, a scout with Forrest's cavalry. In order of presentation, the characters are as follows: Metcalfe, Fountain, Dade, Flickner, Polly, the Squad, and finally Metcalfe's reprise. The first six monologues make three mutually illuminating contrasts with implications as to the antagonistic national characters and interests. Moreover, Foote has provided a variety of links among the monologues, insuring unity and the final effect, namely, "the first great modern battle" as human experience.

Walter Fountain, like Palmer Metcalfe on the Confederate side, is a junior officer who has had opportunity for insight into his commanding general and other superiors. Coming from the same town as U.S. Grant, he knows all the gossip. Otherwise, he is as unlike Metcalfe as North was unlike South. At thirty-two, he is a middle-class civilian through and through, uxorious, stolidly unenthusiastic about military life. Foote presents him on duty as Officer of the Day, doing "as efficient a job as I knew how" although he had protested the assignment to his colonel on the grounds that he needed his sleep in order to do his proper desk work well. His regiment is in camp at Pittsburg Landing by the Tennessee River. He is writing a letter to his wife, excerpts from which are interspersed in his monologue, after making the final rounds of the men on guard at four in the morning. Returning to the guard tent and as near as might be to his own unmilitary character, he had "trimmed the lamp wick, arranged the things on the table, and sat down to write my letter" (33, 34). The contrast between the kinds of literary activity Fountain and Metcalfe engage in the night before the battle tells much about the two characters and the causes they represent.

Fountain can remember from his boyhood in Georgetown, Ohio, how the general under whom he now serves was nicknamed Useless Grant. He is therefore in a position to speak knowledgeably of the alcoholic ne'er-do-well's recent transformation into Unconditional Surrender Grant. As a participant in the Middle Tennessee campaigns where Grant had begun to make his reputation, Fountain can report the difficulties Grant had with his commander, Halleck, until the latter's doubts about Grant's competence and jealousy of his results in the field were resolved. Fountain's regiment having been attached to W. T. Sherman's division, he was witness also to the emergence of Sherman as a credible commander. The preceding November, Sherman had been removed from command on suspicion of insanity, and Fountain's impressions were not reassuring when he first saw the restored commander. In action, however, "Sherman was not the same man at all," and Fountain attests that he and the other men under his command became "willing to follow wherever he said go" (42).

Metcalfe and Fountain having conveyed, incidentally to their personal ruminations, the strategic plans of both sides, the narrative moves to Private Luther Dade. As a native of Jordan County, he is a link to Foote's other fictions. His grandson, Luther Eustis, is the protagonist of *Follow Me Down*. Luther Dade seems to have a special importance for Shelby Foote, who has given him the maiden name of his own great-grandmother, Mary Dade Foote. The name recurred as his father's and his own middle name. Luther, a touching innocent at seventeen, comes from the end of the social scale opposite Palmer Metcalfe's and so amplifies the novel's presentation of Southern attitudes. He has no access to the Napoleonic battle order and little comprehension of the ideology it in part expressed. He is mystified when, on the day the battle was to begin, the sun rises big and red and he hears it hailed as the sun of Austerlitz. The phrase registered with him as "'the sun of oyster itch' whatever that meant" (65–66).

Not that Luther does not receive a version of the battle order Metcalfe helped put in rhetorical trim. He hears three versions, in fact, the first from his colonel. "I didnt understand it much," Luther says, "because what the colonel said was full of tactics talk." His captain explains, "and that was better but not much." Finally, his sergeant explains by drawing lines on the ground with a stick—"That way it was clear as could be" (68). Thus by perfect narrative economy the reader is made to recall Metcalfe's wondering whether the plans that worked so well on the flat clean paper would work out that way on the ground, and Luther is marched off into the maelstrom which his innocence is no more prepared for than Metcalfe's only comparative sophistication is.

Luther's monologue carries the reader through the terrors of the actual battle on the ground, which he steadfastly fights until wounded and forced to seek medical aid, and is followed by Otto Flickner's. As a private in the Union army, Flickner is more cynical than Luther and carries a very different pack of attitudes. Foote introduces Flickner as he joins the thousands of Union skulkers who have fled the field and are seeking shelter under the river bluffs. He assures a fellow coward, "I aint scared the way you made out. . . . I'm what they call demoralized" (97). Much of his monologue is given to rationalizing his behavior under fire.

Whereas Luther Dade could make little enough of "the sun of oyster itch," Flickner has associations with the name of Napoleon which contribute to his "demoralization." He was brought up on tales of "how my granddaddy had fought against Napoleon in the old country"— Germany. To him, the second-generation immigrant, "it seemed so wrong, so out of place, hearing about Napoleon, when I could see right through the living-room window the big rolling Minnesota prairie . . ." (112). But other qualities emerge in Flickner as he mills about with the skulkers and sees the Union reinforcements under General Buell arrive by boat and disembark, shouting scornfully at the retreaters.

Flickner does not yet know that his nerve had broken under sufficient strain: the engagement from which he had fled was what came to be known as the Hornets Nest, which helped set the precedent for a new level of intensity. Victory, had they but realized it, was within the

Confederates' reach pending arrival of the Union reinforcements. Flickner confesses to himself that he "wasnt demoralized back there at the sunken road. . . . I was just plain scared" (120). This self-knowledge is more than he can tolerate. He sets out to search the field and rejoin his outfit, only to learn that his whole division was taken prisoner at about the time he fled, but then stumbles upon his battery, which had escaped, and is accepted.

The fifth and sixth monologues, comprising the third Confederate-Union diptych, inferentially emphasize the distinction between the romantic individualism of the agrarian South and the collectivism of the industrial North. The Confederate term of the comparison is Sergeant Polly, who, as a scout for Forrest's cavalry, is a type of the loner both by nature and by function. He had from the beginning the inclination to "enlist under Forrest" in the symbolic sense of this phrase which develops in the younger Metcalfe as a response to disaster. We meet Polly as he stands on an Indian mound in the midst of the thunderstorm that broke over Shiloh the night of the day following the Hornets Nest, looking down on the arrival of Buell's force.

Knowing that the Confederate chance for victory depends on finishing the engagement before Buell can bring his men into play, Polly finds Forrest and brings him to the mound. Forrest takes a good look: "He knew something had to be done before daylight" (134). He sets out without a word to locate his superiors and urge an immediate attack. Again the reader experiences a tour of the field, as he has in company of Luther Dade seeking medical attention and Flickner his battery, through a very different character propelled by his own kind of urgency.

Part of Polly's function in the novel is to provide a view of Forrest, as Metcalfe is in a position to convey impressions of Johnston, Beauregard, and Sherman, and Fountain of Grant and Sherman. Tough and hardbitten, Polly had been kicked out of divinity school, broken with his Baptist father, and made his way around the world in various rough trades prior to the war. He thought of trying a reconciliation with his father but, having worked as a seaman, decides instead to join the Confederate Navy. He happens while passing through Memphis to see an advertisement calling for enlistments in Forrest's cavalry and decides that is for him. He feels confirmed in his decision and oriented in life on meeting Forrest: "I knew I was looking at the most man in the world." Polly's monologue carries the reader with Forrest on through the battle. Unable to persuade the generals to attack in the night while Buell is vulnerable, Forrest leads his men on with unflagging energy. "We fought them mounted," Polly says, "we fought them dismounted, standing or running, all over that blasted field where the dead lay thick as leaves at harvest time" (150, 158).

The Squad which speaks the collective monologue, if the seemingly contradictory terms may be collocated, is part of the Indiana division under Lew Wallace. The order in which the constituent speeches is presented functions in the same way as order of presentation does in integrating all seven monologues comprising the novel. Private Robert Winter, who speaks first, having been adopted from a Boston orphanage by an Indiana family, is sensitive to the "accidental" quality of human relations. He muses on the strangeness of the twelve lives now melded into that of the squad although "every one of the twelve had his own particular story." It is this youth, whom we have already quoted, who thinks that a book about war, to be correct, would have to take into account all the individual experiences and cannot, therefore, be written: "It would be too jumbled" (164).

But Sergeant Bonner, who speaks next, gives part of the reason why war can be fought and books written about it with some approximation to truth. His key line is: "I got the squad organized." Otherwise, his function is to convey the Union plans for resuming the battle with Buell's troops now in place. Bonner gets a glimpse of Grant conferring with Wallace and prepares to lead the squad into the fray. There is a tense period of waiting while artillery exchanges take place. As the action develops, other men convey the details they experience in the growing confusion. Members of the squad are killed or wounded. What the survivors keep hearing from Bonner is the cry, "Lets form! Lets form!" (169, 173).

The most reflective member of the squad, to whom Foote has assigned the central speech in the series, is Corporal Blake. His status as *raisonneur* is established by allusions to his comments in the first and final speeches. It was he who suggested to Robert Winter during the march to the scene of battle that a book about war ought to tell what each individual "saw in our own little corner." After the battle, when Winter and another man are dead and two other members of the squad wounded, Pope, a shaken survivor, asks himself what his comrades died for and "the answer came back . . . like a voice in the night: *They died for nothing."* Pope then recalls another voice, that of Corporal Blake, who had puzzled everybody two months earlier, after six men were killed at Fort Donelson, by declaring that "the rebels were really on our side." Blake had explained that the rebels "wanted the same things we wanted, the right kind of life, the right kind of government—all that—but theyd been misled by bad men. When they learned the truth they would stop fighting . . ." (164, 191, 192).

Corporal Blake's steady rationality is probably a reflection of Shelby Foote's, and the novelist had evidently a choice to make. If there was to be a seventh and concluding monologue, Corporal Blake might reasonably have been assigned it instead of Lieutentant Metcalfe and the final effect would have been very different. The novel would have ended on a note of sober accommodation rather than with Metcalfe's resolution to "enlist under Forrest," implying not only the continuing intransigence of the South but values other than and maybe higher than rationality. Foote's decision to make this a specifically Southern novel by giving Metcalfe the last word leaves the reader with some thinking to do. Corporal Blake himself saw the absurdity of attempting a God's-eye-view of war and, by implication, of life—in that case, is Metcalfe in spite of everything still merely misled by a bad man, or is there something to be said for passionate enlistment under what one perceives as "the most man in the world" so long as God's view is inaccessible?

The seven parts of *Shiloh* are so nearly self-contained that each is intelligible in isolation, yet Foote has integrated them into a novel. He has done so by evoking place through the different sensibilities and experiences of his characters and then by supplying links, discreet but effectual, among the monologues. The reader, who hears what all the characters have to say, knows more, finally, than any of them could during and immediately after the battle. It is the reader, subtly prompted by the author, who gets the feel of the situation, makes connections, and infers whatever he can as to meanings on the basis of evidence more complete than is available to the characters.

Foote conveys the geography both abstractly, as it appears, for example, on the maps Metcalfe studies before the battle, and empirically as the characters march, fight, fall, or flee on the actual ground. The terrain is, of course, looked at from the points of view of the opposing armies, each of which intends to use it to its own advantage. At the beginning, the armies are almost evenly matched in numbers.

The Confederates think they have caught the Union army between two creeks with its back to the Tennessee River where it can be destroyed, but the Union generals expect nearly to double their force when Buell arrives and blast their way out.

From Metcalfe's monologue emerges a general description of the whole field, while from Fountain's one gets a close look at the initial position of the Union forces. Though doubtful about this on first arriving, he soon realizes "what a good, strong position Sherman had chosen." The creeks, which Metcalfe thinks will trap the Yankees, are seen by Fountain as protecting their flanks while "through the opening to the southwest we had a straight shot for Corinth" (44–45).

Throughout, Foote evokes the changeable April weather as a unifying ambience. The characters variously comment and react, and the reader absorbs their different impressions until he has a sensible experience of the place at the given time. The night before the battle, for example, is clear with a thin moon, which shines at that suspenseful midnight in the eyes of one character after another and is noted in their varying tones and diction. Metcalfe, preparing to sleep in his blanket by the campfire at Johnston's headquarters, observes, "The moon, which had risen in the daylight sky, was as thin as a paring, a sickle holding water but unclouded. I never saw the moon so high, so remote—a dead star lighting a live one where forty thousand men, young and old but mostly young, slept on their arms in line of battle. . . . " Then Fountain, going grumpily about his duties as O.D.: "There was a high thin moon and all the stars were out. However, after the moon went down at half past twelve you couldnt see your hand in front of your face." Then Luther Dade, lying down to sleep "in what they call Line of Battle": "When I went to sleep the stars were out and there was even a moon, thin like a sickle and clear against the night, but when I woke up there was only the blackness . . . " (25, 33, 63).

The monologues are linked for the reader as the characters chance to cross each other's path or observe from their different points of view a particular scene. One after another these incidents register with the reader, in whose mind the novel takes form. Increments of understanding occur as the reader hears first the subjective statement of a given character and then a view of him by another. For example, Palmer Metcalfe, in the opening paragraph of the novel, gives a good-humored

account of himself bringing up the rear of Johnston's cavalcade riding to
the scene of the battle while the infantrymen jeer, "Jog on, sonny. If
you lose him youll never find him again!" (4).

It happens that Luther Dade witnesses this episode and conveys it
with a difference. He says, "There was a little blond-headed lieutenant
bringing up the rear, the one who would go all red in the face when the
men guyed him. . . . He looked about my age, but that was the only
thing about us that was alike. He had on a natty uniform: bobtail
jacket, red silk neckerchief, fire-gilt buttons, and all. I said to myself, I
bet his ma would have a fit if she could see him now" (69–70). This says
much—to emphasize only one aspect, it says something about Southern homogeneity, despite class differences, as the simple country boy
Luther responds to Metcalfe's dash and glamour.

After Luther's monologue concludes, the reader gains two objective
views which both develop Luther's experience of the battle and help
insure the cohesion of the monologues. Sergeant Polly, during the
night when Forrest is trying to warn the Southern commanders of
Buell's arrival and persuade them to attack, happens to notice "a
tow-headed boy wearing a homespun shirt under his jacket. . . . He
was about seventeen, just beginning to raise some fuzz on his cheeks.
He carried his left arm across his stomach. . . . The sleeve of the hurt
arm was caked with blood. . . ." The boy, whom the reader of course
recognizes as Luther, asks where a doctor can be found; Polly gives such
directions as he can and compassionately comments, "He was sad to see:
had a dazed look around the eyes, as if he'd seen things no boy ought to
see . . ." (141).

In very few words, the author has accomplished a number of things.
Metcalfe's red silk and fire-gilt before the battle have been contrasted
with Luther's bloody homespun at the crisis of it, for example. During
the Confederate retreat, Metcalfe becomes aware of Luther. Hanging on
to the tailgate of a wagon for such propulsion as it gives him in his tight
Jeanpris riding boots, Metcalfe notices "a boy in the rear of the wagon;
he looked out over the tailgate, our heads on a line less than a yard
apart. He wore a checkered homespun shirt which was half gone
because of the way the surgeons had slit it when they took off his left
arm. . . ." Gusts of rain and sleet and hail help bring Luther to, and
Metcalfe reports that "for the first time, except for the raving, he
spoke"—he asks, "Lieutenant—did we get whupped?" (196, 222).

The two characters have been given minimal but sufficient rounding, and the novel its final trussing.

Another cross-referencing occurs between the monologues of Otto Flickner and Sergeant Polly, providing—by inference as always—the extreme Yankee and Rebel views of the critical hour when the Union reinforcements are debarking from their river steamers. It is night, with lightning flashing, as Polly looks down on the thousands of Union soldiers who have retreated to the bluffs. If he had not witnessed the fight Union troops put up at the Hornets Nest, where Flickner's battery was in the hottest fire, Polly remarks that he would have concluded "the war couldnt last another week, not with men like those wearing the uniform. I felt almost ashamed for them, because after all it was once our country too" (133). This orchestrates Flickner, who, as the reader knows from his earlier monologue, is just at this instant feeling shame for himself and resolving to rejoin the battle. Then it is Flickner who provides a link back to Fountain, for it is Flickner who hears one of the men who had been on guard duty say that a shell landed in Fountain's lap as he sat in the tent writing his letter to his wife. The reader realizes that Fountain was interrupted by death halfway through the word "love."

It is of considerable interest to the critic that, when Foote completed *Shiloh*, he was by no means finished with the subject; for he rewrote this material as history in the first volume of *The Civil War* some years later. The two versions invite consideration of narrative as a technique applicable both to fiction and to history, especially since it appears that the research for *Shiloh* proved adequate, with little or no supplementation, for the treatment in *The Civil War*. The most material difference between the two versions is that *Shiloh*, for all its economy, is a little more than twice as long as the treatment of the battle in the history. The "facts," down almost to the last detail, are the same in both versions although somewhat compressed by subordination in the inclusive narrative of the whole war. What is additional in the novel is just the fiction, easily analyzable by comparison.

The fictional element consists of the invented characters and the deployment of the historical material through their several points of view together with the cross-referencing of the monologues just described. The author never speaks in his own voice in *Shiloh*, but he is frankly the teller of the tale in *The Civil War*—frankly, but artistically nevertheless, as we shall be at pains to show in the following chapter. The section on the battle of Shiloh in *The Civil War* is the novel recast in the author's voice and strictly limited to material citable in his sources.

# Chapter Six
# A Narrative History

In baldly posting *A Narrative* as the subtitle of his imposing history, *The Civil War,* Shelby Foote advanced a claim for literary sensibility and art in a field where the palms were going to analysis and schemes of quantification and narrative had come to be regarded as intellectually suspect. If the author of a history was to be candidly present in his work, it must be rather as a theorist with some reinterpretation of received views to offer and argue than as a man and an artist. Foote advertised not merely narrative, but *a* narrative, and did so, moreover, as an amateur in the field who had no apologies to make to the professionals. He was relying on professional credentials, but as a writer. He was suggesting that a work of narrative history must be analyzable as that of an identifiable writer, over and above whatever pretensions he might have to original research and methodological rigor, and submitting his book for judgment not just as history but also as art.

## The Response of Critics and Historians

Foote's production of history defined as literature not only placed him athwart professional opinion among historians but also cost him the attention of literary critics, who tend to ignore the claims of nonfiction genres. For a work of its quality and magnitude, *The Civil War* has not received due consideration although there are signs that this situation is changing. The historical journals either ignored or noticed only briefly and condescendingly the first two volumes, but upon the appearance of the third and final accorded high praise to the whole work. We shall examine this shift in opinion below since it relates to serious issues in historiography and is important to the proper recognition of *The Civil War.*

Literary critics and scholars, with several notable exceptions,[1] have shown little awareness of this novelist's application of novelistic technique in history while scrupulously maintaining the distinction between the genres. The general view of Foote in this quarter is probably exemplified by the passing reference to him in the *Harvard Guide to Contemporary American Writing* as one of a group of writers who unfortunately "have allowed the writing of fiction to assume a smaller role in their careers than they may have intended."[2] Historians and literary critics alike have been inclined to take it for granted that, as a reviewer of the first volume of *The Civil War* said, "The shoemaker should stick to his last, the novelist to his fiction."[3]

Foote's challenge to the prejudices of professional and academic historians was the greater in that he wrote what is often deprecated as "mere" military history. The academics, C. Vann Woodward observed in a review of *The Civil War,* not only honor "the analytical urge" while tending to dismiss "the narrative impulse"; they ignore "the strictly martial, guns-and-battle aspect of war, the most essential aspect." Woodward says that historians tend to think that battle action does not yield much "insight" or "clues to mass motivation, keys to puzzles of grand strategy and policy, and answers to large questions of 'why.'"[4] Academic propriety is likely to look askance at rousing action narrative, however scholarly, since it is almost by definition a story of individual human experiences too particularized, however historical, to bear the weight of impressive generalization.

It happened that two other multi-volume treatments of the Civil War, one by Bruce Catton and the other by Allan Nevins, appeared while Foote was engaged with his. In a notice of Foote's second volume which appeared in the *American Historical Review,* the reviewer declared by way of preface, "The scholarship, keen interpretations, and valuable analyses of Nevins place his writings in a superior class of their own"—Nevins being the professionals' professional in the group. The reviewer then stated, "Where Catton and Foote are concerned, however, one can grasp real comparative tangibles." It was a mark of their common inferiority that Catton and Foote concentrated on battles and seemed less at ease in dealing with the political and social aspects of the war. Both seemed biased to this reviewer, Catton pro-Union and Foote pro-Confederate, while Nevins, by implication, remained superbly above the battle. Catton had at least written up a real historian's research, that of his collaborator, E. B. Long, and so had the grace to use some unpublished sources. The reviewer evidently regarded Foote's work as gratuitous since his "main concern is to tell a good, full, and familiar story in as interesting a way as possible."[5] The notice was an explanation of why it was not worth reviewing—or, dare we infer, even reading—and no review followed.

In an annotated bibliography of writing on the Civil War which appeared when Foote and Nevins were still in process of publishing their treatments and Catton had published all of his, the ranking recurs: Nevins in a class by himself as a proper historian; Catton and Foote, both regarded as mere writers, but Catton nearer the mark than Foote. The terms of the notations are revealing. Nevins's work is described: "Two deeply analytical volumes . . . marked by such thorough research and scholarship that the volumes will stand for years at the peak of Civil War history." As for Catton, his book was said to be "one of the outstanding literary achievements of the Centennial years; Catton here demonstrates his prodigious ability to tell a story well without neglecting detail." The generic distinction between scholarly analysis and storytelling is clear, the latter redeemed to some extent by attention to "detail." Of Foote's work, all that was noted was that " . . . this panoramic military study is written in a sweeping style."[6] Our account of *The Civil War* below should sufficiently indicate the impertinence of this comment. Here, the pejoratives "panoramic," "military," and "sweeping" should be noted as characteristic of language conventionally employed in adverse criticism of narrative history.

Surprisingly, the review of Foote's third volume carried by the *American Historical Review* pronounces that this completes a work "leaving us richer in new literature and historical narrative" of the Civil War. Foote is now promoted to equality with Allan Nevins, Bruce Catton, and Carl Sandburg, praised for his rendering of "complexities" and contingencies, admired for the vividness of his treatment of battles, and credited with "a style that remains warm and consistently human." He is allowed his Southern point of view and even excused for having "depended heavily upon the secondary materials." The reviewer reveals lingering professional uneasiness: "Though history written as literature may cease to be history as we should define it, it may still retain validity as an art form and as another source." But he ends with the remark that Foote's book "reminds us that history can be presented with beauty and feeling and be written for understanding."[7]

Some of the reasons behind this shift in the professional historians' judgment of Foote's work are suggested by a review of all three volumes by the authority who had been dismissive in the notice of Volume II in the *American Historical Review.* James I. Robertson, Jr., writing in *Civil War History,* mounted what was in effect a handsome apology in the name of the profession. Acknowledging that "a feeling persists that the study of history is slipping into a closed shop exclusively for the professionals" and that "such an occurrence would be disastrous for all concerned," he names several writers whose studies have shown "that history can be human, appealing at all levels, and enjoyable if the narrator can use a broad base and a gifted pen." Foote is said to exemplify these attributes in "brilliant fashion" and to rank "as one of the half-dozen major figures in Civil War writing."[8]

Robertson supposes that "punctilious" historical scholars will nevertheless attack Foote's book because of "his total reliance on printed sources," his refusal to supply footnotes, his "aversion to making interpretations," and his saying "little not already well-known and readily accessible in other works." The reviewer can find excuses for Foote on all of these counts except one—the missing footnotes. He still must have these although he has become unusual among historians reviewing history in his application of the criteria of literary criticism as well as those of "scientific" history. Some of his judgments of Foote's work may be faulted as literary criticism, of whose theory and principles he seems to have only a limited grasp, but he roundly declares that "what sustains these three volumes—what Foote utilizes that others missed—is a prose ranging from powerful to adroit." Noting that the major American historical journals ignored the first two volumes, he states that now the set is complete, "Foote no longer can be, or will be, ignored."[9]

## Validity of Narrative History

The doubts about the validity of narrative history among professional historians, which have delayed appreciation of Foote's work, descend from the end of the nineteenth century when history was organized as a profession with pretensions to status as a social science. Earlier the United States had produced a great generation of "Romantic Historians"—George Bancroft, John Lothrop Motley, Francis Parkman; but with the introduction of doctoral programs based on a Germanic model, a new objectivity was demanded. Oscar Handlin observes that these new pretensions required the repudiation of the idea that history "achieved its goals, as did other forms of literature, by emphasis upon the narrative; [that] the story chronologically told supplied its own organization and permitted the component parts of the whole to fall into their appropriate places." Historians who would be scientists felt that writers of narrative history, with a few exceptions such as Francis Parkman and Edward Eggleston, "evaded many problems of organization and interpretation" with the result that "simple conceptions of motivation and causation were the usual features of the narrative form."[10]

Handlin added that the scientific historians, with a professional interest to protect, decided that history must no longer be "the avocation of gentlemanly scholars, journalists, and litterateurs, working as individuals"—just so, we surmise, many professional historians must regard Shelby Foote. The scientific historians prided themselves on a rigorous "technique of handling facts" and felt that writers of narrative history typically "fixed on the large sweep of history" and "had often been casual in matters of detail."[11] Here are some of the very terms we have seen used in connection with Foote, suggesting that a stereotype has been applied to him.

The upshot of the development Handlin describes was that professional, academically qualified historiography "shifted from loose discursive narrative to the heavily footnoted monograph focused on a clearly defined problem." A naive idea of narrative as by definition loose and discursive and probably uncritically subjective as well seems to have taken unwarranted hold. Moreover—and here again Foote as a highly individual talent falls athwart professional attitudes—professionalism meant preference for "the collaborative series . . . in which specialists pooled their talents."[12]

If Foote has seemed to be a throwback to the preprofessional days, he has also proved unassimilable to trends in professional history since the decline of its aspirations to scientific rigor. By the time volume 3 of *The Civil War* was published, fashion had shifted away even from the scientific historian's article of faith that "the fact was absolutely intractable." Foote, scholarly gentleman and litterateur though he might be, never abandoned this article and so must seem doubly old-fashioned to historians emerging in the 1970s who "regarded the fact itself as malleable." Neither *Shiloh,* avowedly a novel, nor *The Civil War,* announced as narrative, can be categorized as "faction," i.e., as Handlin puts it, "a combination of fact and fiction" in which "the factual elements" are "instrumental to the purpose of the author-manipulator."[13] Foote has consistently resisted this hybrid whether it crops up on the novelist's side of the fence as the popular "historical novel" or the modish "nonfiction novel," or on the historian's as "faction."

The question in the light of which Foote's work as historian should be considered is whether narrative history can be intellectually valid as well as artistically satisfactory. It happens that during the twenty years he worked on *The Civil War* this question, as well as that of the status of military history, was addressed by several scholars. The consensus seems generally rehabilitative with regard to "the narrative impulse" although in no way pejorative with regard to "the analytical urge." The great problem is whether narrative history can be trusted, not merely as to the adequacy and correctness of its factual elements, but also as to the credibility of the conjunctions—ultimately, statements of causal relations between successive events—which it makes between the facts.

There is a prior problem as to the basis on which facts are selected for inclusion, since the selection is unavoidably the result of value-judgments on the part of the historian. Avoiding the paralysis of complete skepticism, Morton White has argued for the doctrine of "existential regularism" or the "covering law theory of explanation" in narrative history, which, though not so strict as the laws of physics and not productive of deductive argument, tends to validate historical narrative conjunction. The historian as a person, his interests, his biases if need be, must be taken into account in judging narrative history. The critic must be prepared to accept that there may be different histories of the same subject, all true but differentiated by the orientation of the several historians, e.g., to political conservatism or liberalism.[14]

W. B. Gallie has made a point about the logic of narrative which will also be found illuminating in assessing *The Civil War*. He argues that "the sense of 'following'—following *to* a conclusion—that applies to stories is of an altogether different kind from the sense of following an argument so that we see that its conclusion *follows*." Stories, including narrative histories, deal in contingencies, not usually regarded as "intellectually acceptable" in philosophy, which tends to believe that to understand is to command. "It is as a corrective to this widespread belief," Gallie asserts, "that an adequate account of what it is to follow a story, or an historical narrative, is of general philosophical importance:

since following, in this sense, provides the most striking case of our use in thought of generalizations, not to command or forestall events, but to find them intellectually acceptable. . . . " He does not think that the purpose of writing history is to prove or disprove scientifically statements about how in general societies function. Rather, he declares, and we infer that Foote must agree, that the function of narrative history is "to enable us to follow the actual course of certain events to a known conclusion, for the sake of the events themselves and their direct human interest, quite apart from whatever exemplification of scientific truths or accepted truisms they may afford."[15]

Gallie is again illuminating when he compares the historian's explanations (that is, the way he selects and establishes relations among the facts) to those of an expert explaining the moves in a game. The historian's explanations are aids in following "a developing performance or game or story or history." They differ from applying generalizations in order to predict or deduce a future event, a procedure which enables "us to dispense with observation." Gallie denies that the historian must "believe in the deducibility of any and every human historical event from certain laws and certain earlier existing conditions."[16] The historian may use contingencies as well as calculable and foreseeable, or logically appraisable, factors in explaining situations and developments. Historical understanding differs from but, in Gallie's view, is not less respectable than scientific understanding.

Especially pertinent to the discussion of Foote's work in the two kinds of narrative, as the title suggests, is Leo Braudy's *Narrative Form in History and Fiction.* Braudy draws some conclusions from analyses of David Hume's *History of England,* Henry Fielding's novels, especially *The History of Tom Jones, A Foundling,* and Edward Gibbon's *The Decline and Fall of the Roman Empire.* These classics date from the eighteenth century, when modern historiography began. The writers took comparable approaches "to such problems as verisimilitude, narrative progression, and thematic development," and all three, according to Braudy, resorted to "the establishment and exploitation of an individual narrative voice and point of view." With regard to Hume's and Gibbon's histories, Braudy is concerned, as we must be with regard to Foote's, "to discern a logic of narrative progression that can account for the artistic unity of each work."[17]

Because Hume conceived of the cause-effect nexus as consisting only in continuity in time and contiguity in space, Braudy observes that he still had the old annalists' problem of dealing with one-thing-after-another: how to provide for selection, emphasis, and continuity in some logically coherent manner. Complicating this issue for Hume was his ideal of the historian as an impersonal observer. He attempted to vary the dullness of merely chronological recital—history as dates—by introducing character sketches of important personages and by providing appendices in which he discussed social and cultural topics. Braudy believes, however, that his narrative method was flawed because "he does not speak enough in his own voice. He sacrifices more complete and possibly more interesting coherences because he appears to believe that a recognizable point of view automatically means bias and distortion. . . ."[18]

In the meantime, Fielding developed in fiction about the private history of an individual a narrative method which Gibbon was able to adapt for the purposes of public history of an empire. Like historians, Fielding and other novelists "sought to form time, to discover its plot, and to give a compelling and convincing narrative shape to the facts of human life, whether observed directly or through the records and 'memorials' of the past." In such a fictional work as *Tom Jones,* Fielding writes the "clear, but ultimately personal, perceptions of an individual confronting a specific situation" and avoids both "the excessive subjectivity of romance and the excessive objectivity of public history." Instead of creating a character or an assumed omniscience to serve as narrator of his history, Gibbon creates a narrative voice which is essentially his own. He does not claim that there is an innate pattern in the past which he is objectively describing. Rather, he produces a work of literary art, using the past as material but imposing upon it a candidly provisional coherence. This coherence comprises what one identifiable, perceptive individual can make of the past, so that "the shape of history [or, one might more clearly say, of events] in the *Decline and Fall* is pre-eminently a construction, a literary work with aesthetic rather than systematic order and coherence."[19]

Braudy argues that "Gibbon synthesizes in his work such contrasting benefits as Hume's ironic detachment and Fielding's individual but authoritative narrative voice, Hume's emphasis on the body of established law and Fielding's praise of individual vitality, Hume's strict chronology and Fielding's frequently associative flow of events, digressions, and meditations." The indispensable element in Gibbon's method is the establishment of his own "authoritative narrative voice," and we shall argue that this is also the key to Foote's work in the historical kind and that he learned how to do it by writing novels. The goal is detachment without depersonalization, which "involves . . . our sense of the capabilities of the person who is being subjective" in narrating events.[20]

The credibility of the artistically controlled narrative voice in history must be established first upon scholarship and documentation but no less upon plentiful evidence of sensitivity to human nature. Foote, having established his narrative voice, was freed, as Braudy argues Gibbon was, to reduce stress upon chronology, sometimes to alter it, moving in foreshadowings and flashbacks and associations, digressing, making connections between one place or period and another.[21]

## The Status of Military Narrative History

Before turning to Foote's own remarks on these matters, we should look more particularly to the question of the status of military narrative history. In his review of *The Civil War* quoted above, Woodward admits that narration of the killing in battles, however brilliant artistically, may not be relevant to the concerns of "psychohistorians," "cliometricians," and "crypto-analysts." He thinks, however, that Foote's work "might serve to expose them to the terrifying chaos and mystery of their intractable subject and disabuse them of some of their illusions of mastery."[22]

The discussion of military historiography which seems most applicable to *The Civil War* is John Keegan's *The Face of Battle,* in which one may learn both the basis of prejudice against battle narratives and principles on which this subgenre "could reasonably hope to achieve either the autonomy of an academic discipline or the aesthetic freedom of genuine literature." Keegan traces the prejudice against the genre among English-speaking critics, at least, to cultural ambivalence about conflict and aggression. How to justify relish for the vivid telling of butchery (to adapt a phrase of Woodward's) or (as Keegan says) "any discussion of war which did not condemn it outright as an aberration on the face of human history"?[23]

Keegan argues that the problem was rationalized by what he calls "the Decisive Battle idea," i.e., the idea that battles make a major difference and even improve the human situation. The result has been "a dispensation," dating from a Victorian best-seller, Edward Creasy's *Fifteen Decisive Battles of the World* (1851), permitting "endless, repetitive examination of battles which by no stretch of the imagination can be said to have done anything but make the world worse." Allowed "to wallow in battles for battles' sake," many writers have been able "to evade any really inquisitive discussion of what battles might be like by recourse to the easy argument that one must stick to the point, which is decision, results, winning or losing."[24]

Another source of doubt as to the intellectual and aestheic propriety of military history has been the prominence of what Keegan calls "the battle piece" among products of the kind. He says the chief model for it has been Caesar's *Commentaries* but points to an alternative and preferable tradition stemming from Thucydides, whom Foote has mentioned among his own models. Keegan notes with approval Michael Grant's statement of the difference between Roman and Greek military historiography: the former "began with politics and the state," the latter "sprang from geography and human behaviour."[25] Foote certainly takes the Greek way, so defined; the point is emphasized by his echoes of the epic tone of Homer in rendering battle.

## Foote: The Novelist as Historian

In order to appreciate Foote's approach in history-writing—battle history, at that—the terms of the discussion must expand to accommodate the art of writing as well as philosophy of history and the practice of professional historians. Foote is correct and even diffident in speaking of the work of the professionals and scrupulous in acknowledging debts to it. He has asserted that the honest novelist and historian both seek to write the truth of events whether imaginative or worldly and that neither can dispense with either kind. Both, he believes, desire "to tell us *how it was*" but by "their separate methods," which are not, however, absolutely different. The chief difference is that "the historian attempts this by communicating facts, whereas the novelist would communicate sensation. The one stresses action, the other *re*-action."[26] Writing history, a novelist is no more free than the professional historian to skimp or distort facts. He will write narrative but it will be "evidenced" narrative (to adopt a usage employed by Gallie). The implication is, however, that in selecting facts the novelist-as-historian will be inclined to include many that either report or evoke sensation.

Foote is insistent that the historian as well as the novelist must master the technique of writing and develop a style. He will not excuse the historian from achieving "command of language." The historian must, no less than the novelist, arrrive at "a way of looking at the world: Proust called it 'a quality of vision.'" He has commented that historians tend not to develop themselves as "serious writers" and that "all too many of them not only *prefer* to skip this sweatshop apprenticeship; they *do* skip it." In his opinion, historians are usually at their worst and most partial in "the treatment of character" because they tend to document an opinion and to judge instead of doing a proper (novelistic) job of characterization informed with sympathetic understanding. "It is here that the historian most gravely violates the novelist's canon. . . . Even if his purpose is destruction—which I deplore—the historian does wrong to go about it in this way: as any novelist could tell him. The proper and effective way to accomplish the destruction of a man is to show him sympathy, and in the course of showing that sympathy, permit the man himself to show that it is undeserved."[27]

Foote feels that historians also tend to fail in "the management of *plot*." He takes it for granted that history, in the sense of a written account, must be plotted, regardless of views as to whether actual events of the past may be said to have had an inherent plot. The plotting of history includes the "arrangement of events in dramatic sequence," calculation of "the amount of space and stress each of these events is to be accorded," and calibration of the rate and timing of the release of information. Technically accomplished plotting gives a book, history as well as fiction, "its larger rhythms and provides it with narrative drive, the force that makes it move under its own power." Plotting also involves for the historian decisions as to what to leave out, and Foote suggests an analogy with painting, especially Vermeer's. The desideratum is clarity of presentation, suggesting sometimes what is not presented. "The drama comes from where the picture starts and stops; from where it meets the frame." As in his fiction, Foote also uses in *The Civil War* and thinks historians should normally use arrangements of events analogous to musical forms such as the sonata and the fugue: "we need all the help we can get, whether as writers or as readers," and patterns analogous to music allow for the forecasting, presentation, and repetition with variation of material. In short, Foote is firm in the view that "there is no reason why the historian should not be an artist, too."[28]

Foote has gone so far as to say that history, "in my handling of it, is another style of novel—that is, not with any fiction in it but an exercise very similar to the writing of novels." This was probably a hyperbolic remark, made in the course of an interview, which professional historians would no doubt find extreme unless they saw that the emphasis fell on the technique of writing. The genres are discriminated, after all, primarily by the presence or absence of fiction; and Foote stated in the same interview, "There's something about mixing fact and fiction that goes against my grain."[29]

While asserting truth to be the goal of both novel and history, Foote believes that history, no less than the novel, is "at its best . . . an approximation." For him there is no blinking the subjective element in both, which must be under artistic control in both. He has said that in history "my truth would be different from yours. And mine would be read as mine, and yours would be read as yours. And it would be absorbed by someone who would—absorb both of them and put them together and come up with a third truth."[30]

Foote says that as a writer of narrative history he wants "to know how it was," whereas a writer of historical monograph—the form usually accorded the greater respect by professionals—"is generally concentrating on explaining some action, the consequences of it, how it began, what it did, and what came of it."[31] Knowing what the human experience felt like involves imagining past events as developing process, replete with contingencies, and requires, therefore, the narrative form. The monograph is an account of past events as accomplished facts, winnowed from the contingencies, and requires the form of exposition. The implication seems to be that the function of historical monograph is to be absorbed as an element of narrative history—which *is* history. It is only a recent prejudice which rates the monograph (to say nothing of the revisionist polemic) higher and sneers at "synthesis."

Expounding the elements common to writing novels and writing history, Foote has said, "I don't know of anything I learned about the writing of novels in the course of practicing my craft that's not applicable to the writing of history." Both novelist and historian deal with facts, the novelist getting his out of his head and the historian getting his out of documents. There is no question for Foote either of the novelist being less true to his facts than the historian is to his, or of the novelist-turned-historian being irresponsibly subjective or sensational in handling documented material. "Many people think that a novelist, trying to write history, would distort the facts." But Foote adds with quiet emphasis, "He is not accustomed to distorting facts. . . . what we're really talking about is the technique he learned as a novelist. I claim that all his techniques are applicable."[32]

In *The Civil War* Foote sought to control "the rush of time's multiplicity," as Braudy said Gibbon attempted to do in the *Decline and Fall,* by relying upon "the firmness of his own point of view and an almost

Virgilian sense of the existence of a geographic site through time."[33]
The point of view in question remains that of a cultivated Deltan, as we
have explained, its firmness and definition increased by his having
deployed it in a somewhat Virgilian treatment of part of the Delta in
the Jordan County fictions. We shall be concerned with analysis of the
authorial point of view in a compassing narrative voice, with the way
that voice plots the events it narrates, and with the way it characterizes
the persons involved in *The Civil War*.

## *The Civil War:* Sources and Methods

First, however, since the credibility of all this depends, in a work of
history, upon the author's scholarhip, we should consider Foote's
sources and his use of them. More than one commentator has suggested
some inadequacy here, generally because Foote relied mainly on published sources and turned up no evidence changing received views. Yet
the purpose of competent publication is to settle the facts, obviate the
necessity for searching unpublished sources, and make the ascertained
material available for synthesis. The published sources on the Civil War
come to an immense total. Was a man to start from scratch? Or should
he be judged, rather, by his industriousness and discrimination in using
accumulated scholarly capital? At all events, Foote, so far as we know,
has never been charged with error.

The bibliographical notes appended to each of the three volumes
indicate that, if *The Civil War* is "only" a synthesis, it is an inclusive
one. There is plentiful evidence that Foote did a great deal of research in
sources qualifying as primary though published and used few unpublished ones. He relied heavily on the words of participants in the war
and their contemporaries, studied photographs—Brady's above all—
and mined the 128-volume *War of the Rebellion: a Compilation of the
Official Records of the Union and Confederate Armies* and the 30-volume
*Official Records of the Union and Confederate Navies in the War of the
Rebellion.* He distinguishes between testimony dating from the war and
later memoirs, regimental histories, and so on, which however he used
with critical care, together with diplomatic correspondence and con-
gressional transcripts. "All else," he notes, "is speculation or sifting, an
attempt to reconcile differences and bring order out of multiplicity by
sorting the fruits that have poured from this horn of plenty." Though
he relied first upon "the first-hand testimony," Foote acknowledges his

use of a rich array of secondary sources both "in their own right" and "as a guide through the labyrinth" (1:813).[34]

In assessing the quality of Foote's research, it is important to understand that it included scrutiny of original documents of another kind, the battlefields. He acknowledges the assistance of the National Park Service in helping him "to get the look and feel of the various battlefields," many of which have been expertly preserved (1:814). Geography, as Keegan insists, is an indispensable element in military history which has sometimes been dispensed with. Foote not only appreciated its importance as a technical requirement of the genre but brought to it the "sense of place" which is one of the distinctions of his Jordan County fictions.

Several points should be kept in mind with regard to Foote's use of his sources. The first, already alluded to, is that he discriminated among documents contemporary with the war, documents reflecting the views of participants after the war, and secondary sources. He kept his research current during the long period required for the production of his book. He acknowledged, in the bibliographical note at the end of volume 2, his debt to the spate of publications which appeared in connection with the centennial observance of the war. On the evidence of the note at the end of volume 3, he took into account everything that appeared to 1974.

A second point is that, while deploying his sources from an identifiable point of view, he has so artfully controlled the narrative voice and balanced the presentation of the opposing forces that the reader is persuaded that nothing is distorted. The tone may be unmistakably Southern, but there is no chauvinism. As we have seen in the Jordan County books, his attitude toward the South, and that part of it that for him is "down home," is anything but sentimental. Such sectional bias as he had to control in writing about the Civil War was decreased during the writing by the racist demagoguery of Ross Barnett, Orval Faubus, and George Wallace, then governors, respectively, of Mississippi, Arkansas, and Alabama. Foote thanks them for reminding him of "much that was least admirable in the position my forebears occupied." Futhermore, he has asserted, "If pride in the resistance my forebears made against the odds has leaned me to any degree in their direction, I hope it will be seen to amount to no more, in the end, than the average American's normal sympathy for the underdog in a fight" (2:971, 1:816).[35]

Crude bias, whether sectional, political, or ideological, being of no concern, the reader may still ask whether *The Civil War* is an exercise in argumentation. Foote asked the question himself at the conclusion and declared that "although nowhere along the line have I had a 'thesis' to argue or maintain—partly no doubt because I never saw one yet that could not be 'proved,' at least to the satisfaction of the writer who advanced it—I did have one thing I wanted to do, and that was to restore a balance I found lacking in nearly all the histories composed within a hundred years of Sumter." He wished to correct a prevalent notion that "the War was fought in Virginia, while elsewhere—in an admittedly large but also rather empty region known vaguely as 'the West'—a sort of running skirmish wobbled back and forth, presumably as a way for its participants, faceless men with unfamiliar names, to pass the time while waiting for the issue to be settled in the East" (3:1064–65). He restores balance by treating the Western campaigns with as much particularity as he devotes to the Eastern ones and by showing how they interacted to produce the final decision in the East.

The third point, and the most crucial, we have of course been aproaching since we began the discussion of *Shiloh*: we must now say something definitive about Foote's frankly novelistic approach in historiography. As a writer who literally outlines his books, novels included, and writes systematically under that governance, he was prepared to address this point before committing himself to write history and had his say in the bibliographical note to volume 1. He took as his cue a warning by a professional historian to the effect that the testimony set down after the war by the Union general Lew Wallace, who became a popular novelist, should be discounted. "Recollections of events long past are always to be suspected," the historian opined, and added sagely, "and especially when set down by a writer of fiction." With patient good humor, Foote confessed, "Well, I am a novelist," and continued:

and what is more I agree with D. H. Lawrence's estimate of the novel as "the one bright book of life." I might also agree with the professor quoted above, but only by considering each witness on his merit, his devotion as a writer to what should be his main concern. The point I would make is that the novelist and the historian are seeking the same thing: the truth—not a different truth: the same truth—only they reach it, or try to reach it, by different routes. Whether the event took place in a world now gone to dust, preserved by documents and evaluated by scholarship, or in the imagination, preserved by memory and distilled by the creative process, they both want to tell us *how it was*: to re-create it, by their separate methods, and make it live again in the world around them.

This has been my aim, as well, only I have combined the two. Accepting the historian's standards without his paraphernalia, I have employed the novelist's methods without his license. Instead of inventing characters and incidents, I searched them out—and having found them, I took them as they were. Nothing is included here, either within or outside quotation marks, without the authority of documentary evidence which I consider sound. Although I have left out footnotes, believing that they would detract from the book's narrative quality by intermittently shattering the illusion that the observer is not so much reading a book as sharing an experience, I have thought it proper to employ the three dots of elision to signify the omission of interior matter from quotations. In all respects, the book is as accurate as care and hard work could make it. Partly I have done this for my own satisfaction; for in writing a history, I would no more be false to a fact dug out of a valid document than I would be false to a "fact" dug out of my head in writing a novel. Also, I have tried for accuracy because I have never known a modern historical instance where the truth was not superior to distortion, by any standard and in every way. Wherever the choice lay between soundness and "color," soundness had it every time. (1:815–16).

We have only to bring out from this credo of the novelist as historian an implication that novels as well as other documents must be expected among the sources of *The Civil War.* They function as sources of method and as aesthetic touchstones rather than as sources of data. He has observed, "Stendhal wrote of war the way he did. Tolstoy learned from Stendhal and added to it. Crane learned from Tolstoy." Alluding to *Shiloh,* he added, "I hope [it is] in that line,"[36] and the remark may be extended to *The Civil War,* behind which Tolstoy in particular seems to be a pervasive presence. Foote has more than once suggested even that historians might also use certain novels as sources of fact. The sources of *The Civil War* include Marcel Proust, who, as Foote has recorded, "taught me more about the organization of material than even Gibbon has done"; and Mark Twain and William Faulkner, "for they left their sign on all they touched, and in the course of this exploration of the American scene I often found that they had been there before me" (2:970–71).

Foote once named Tacitus as his "favorite historian," but he quotes Thomas Hobbes's comment on Thucydides as the "finest compliment" paid a historian. According to Hobbes, "though he never digress to read a Lecture, Moral or Political, upon his own Text, nor enter into men's hearts, further than the Actions themselves evidently guide him . . . [he] filleth his Narrations with that choice of matter, and ordereth them with that Judgement, and with such perspicuity and efficacy expresseth himself that (as Plutarch saith) he maketh his Auditor a Spectator" (2:971).

The source, other than those dealing with the Civil War and the novels and histories which influenced the technique, which has most patently influenced Foote's work is the *Iliad*. He has acknowledged that "Richmond Lattimore's translation of the *Iliad* put a Greekless author in close touch with his model" (2:970). The organization of *The Civil War* parallels that of the *Iliad* and, together with discreet use of such devices as the epic simile and epithet, functions as a pervasive allusion. It is a source of irony as modern instances are played against a general consciousness of antique types and piety which has been maintained in the reader's mind. More importantly, it signals the author's concern with individual men and their experiences of the war in a sort of present-participial, future-conditional mode which conveys a feeling for events as developmental and contingent.

One commentator has elevated this Homeric allusiveness, which we see rather as a technical device, to the status of an "overriding" theme, namely, "that this war like other wars was at once a collision of huge impersonal forces and of highly individuated human beings, that fate and personality co-exist in an indivisible equation. The idea is as old as the *Iliad*."[37] Foote has used the *Iliad* subtly and happily as a way of keeping the reader aware that *The Civil War* is about the actualities of war as they registered here and there and from time to time upon the pulses of living human beings, rather than about what it may be interpreted to mean in general terms.

## *The Civil War:* "Quality of Vision"

The quality of the vision which shapes *The Civil War* and finds the *Iliad* an appropriate touchstone can be described as "Modern"—the informed, disabused vision of a writer who approaches his work as an art to which, far from pretending to impossible detachment, he brings the accidents of his own breeding as part of his materials. The subjective is submitted to the processes of literary art and is thus available to analysis and may be discounted if in any perspective the vision seems near- or

farsighted or astigmatic. We find in Foote's book the formalism—
attention to structure and design, balance, symmetry, proportion—
which distinguishes the great moderns and is a first tenet of modern
criticism. The narrative voice is poised, generous, telling many sides
from many angles and from a late position in a long tradition. This may
be described as humanist, with a Southern quality involving piety real
but rueful and pervasive irony.

Foote added as an epigraph to volumes 2 and 3, as if in writing the
first volume he became persuaded of its appropriateness, a passage from
Ecclesiasticus 44 which seems to signal this mix of piety and irony. The
Old Testament writer praises equally the forebears "that have left a
name behind them . . . and some . . . which have no memorial," for
they are all accounted "merciful men whose righteousness hath not been
forgotten." So far, the note of piety comes clear, and we shall see that
toward the participants in the Civil War Foote's magnanimity is
far-reaching. But when we read further that with the seed of the earlier
generations "shall continually remain a good inheritance and their
children are within the covenant, their seed standeth fast," we pause.
We do, that is, if we read our author's fiction as well as his history and
remember, for example, Major Barcroft of *Love in a Dry Season* or Pauly
Green in "Rain Down Home." Irony does not, even so, undercut piety
altogether in the portrayal of the later generations—in the case, for
instance, of Luther Dade Eustis in *Follow Me Down.*

Foote's complex irony bears family resemblance to that of his elders
who have been grouped as figures in "the Southern Renaissance" and
beyond them to that of other artists and critics usually associated with
literary modernism. A writer with whose attitude toward the world,
the South, and its past Foote feels a strong affinity is John Crowe
Ransom, not the Ransom of *I'll Take My Stand* so much as he "Of the
Mississippi the bank sinister, and of the Ohio the bank sinister," who
said, "Declension looks from our land, it is old."[38] As the Jordan
County fictions attest, Foote hardly qualifies as an uncritical follower of
Agrarianism although he analyzes his county into an agrarian southern
part and an urban-industrial north and sees "declension" in characters
who abandon the one for the other. Declension had no very romantic
height from which to decline. Nevertheless, given the parlousness of
the human condition at all times and places, Foote can appreciate "the
manliness of men" under pressure and understand how this may reveal
cowardice as well as courage, weakness or strength. That phrase is

Ransom's subtitle for the group of poems in which "Antique Harvesters," which we have quoted, appears.

Another mark of the Southern in Foote's history is its exemplification of that specialty of Southern writers, the "sense of place." In *The Civil War,* we find economical, functional use of concrete detail, the sensory effects that anchor the narrative, the human story, to "the world's body"—to use another well-known phrase of Ransom's. "Location," Eudora Welty has observed, "pertains to feeling; feeling profoundly pertains to place; place in history partakes of feeling, as feeling about history partakes of place." She believes that "the exactness and concreteness and solidity of the real world achieved in a story"—and we expand her term to include narrative history—"correspond to the intensity of feeling in the author's mind," and "there lies the secret of our confidence in him." So says Keegan with respect to the criteria of military history. Miss Welty adds that "the sense of place is as essential to good and honest writing as a logical mind" and thinks that "surely they are somewhere related."[39] This relationship could hardly be clearer than in Foote's fiction and history.

We shall digress here to particularize this aspect of *The Civil War* by examining the account Foote gives of the battle of Fredericksburg in December 1862, which occupies pages 20–45 of the second volume. Passages devoted to the geographical relations of the battlefield, its topographical peculiarities, and the meteorological conditions which obtained during the engagement are distributed throughout, serving as warp upon which the woof of narration is woven. The author has also been concerned with historical ties, that is, with the feelings which already pertained to that place, as well as with the influence of the place upon the tactics of the battle.

Fredericksburg was grand "as a spectacle, in which respect it equaled, if indeed it did not outdo, any other major conflict of the war." It was "staged . . . with a curtain of fog that lifted, under the influence of a genial sun, upon a sort of natural amphitheater . . . it quite fulfilled the volunteers' early-abandoned notion of combat as a picture-book affair." The theatrical quality is heightened by allusions to earlier actors upon the scene, such as John Paul Jones, Hugh Mercer, and James Monroe. The reader is reminded that the widowed Mary Washington had lived in the town "and it was here or near here that her son was reported to have thrown a Spanish silver dollar across the Rappahannock."

The main features are quickly established: heights facing each other, town, river, and a stretch of level valley between Union and Confederate armies. The Confederates look down their gun barrels from entrenchments set high on a range of hills; the Union commander Burnside studies the terrain from across the Rappahannock. One terrain, meant to serve two incompatible purposes, its features assessed therefore in different ways, is invested with hope and fear accordingly. Under cover of darkness, the Union army throws a pontoon bridge across the river. The Confederates, "judging by the sound that the pontoniers had reached midstream," open rifle fire, aiming "necessarily by ear. . . . After the first yelp of pain there was the miniature thunder of boots on planks, diminishing as the runners cleared the bridge; then silence, broken presently by the boom-boom of the two guns passing the word along the ridge that the Yanks were coming."

Each morning, the valley is shrouded in fog, so that this battle is remembered for acoustical effects by day as well as by night. Men on both sides had strained to hear what the other might be up to. By late morning or noon the fog had cleared with the repeated effect of a curtain rising to reveal developments. Yet another view is suggested as Foote notes, "High over Stafford Heights, where the long-range guns were adding their deeper voices to the chorus of the Union, two of Burnside's big yellow observation balloons bobbed and floated, the men in their swaying baskets looking down on war reduced to miniature." The bluecoats repeatedly stream across the bridge (and the reader sees them in balloonist's perspective) and up the fatal slopes to test Longstreet's and Jackson's corps as Lee monitors the action from a hilltop.

One night the aurora borealis unexpectedly plays. The next morning "brought a terrestrial phenomenon, equally amazing in its way." The ground in front of a Confederate entrenchment, "formerly carpeted solid blue" with Union bodies, "had taken on a mottled hue, with patches of startling white." Shivering underequipped Confederates had crept out in the night to "scavenge the warm clothes from the bodies of men who needed them no longer."

This situation is used by Foote to introduce a nearer view of this battle which had momentarily reinforced naive recruits (we recall Lieutenant Metcalfe of *Shiloh*) in their illusion that battle was a picture-book affair. He administers an antidote to any tendency to see it as "pageantry." A truce is called by Burnside to bury his dead and rescue his wounded, and the author conducts the reader on a burial detail. "Up close, you heard the groans and smelled the blood. You saw the dead." This is followed by the words of "one who moved among them" and recorded in horror what he experienced.

Such close-textured rendering of particular places is balanced in *The Civil War* by frequent reminders of the total geography of the war as it engulfed the territory of the Confederacy. For example, the section following the narrative of Fredericksburg opens: "Near the far end of the thousand-mile-long firing line that swerved and crooked its way between North and South—westward across northern Virginia, East and Middle Tennessee, North Mississippi, central Arkansas, and thence on out to Texas—Theophilus Holmes, with less rank and not one half as many soldiers in a department better than twenty times as large, had troubles which, in multiplicity at any rate, made Lee's seem downright single" (2:45). This is one of Foote's numerous transitions from campaigns in the East to those in the West, developing what he said is the nearest he comes to a thesis.

It involves rendering what we may call, by adapting Ransom, "the Confederacy's body" and diffuses in the narrative a physical sense of the nation and its suffering. Foote had contemporary license for this device in the Union's "Anaconda" strategy, according to which the Confederacy was to be encircled, crushed, dismembered, and consumed. This larger sense of place is maintained throughout and graphically emphasized by maps showing the contractions of Confederate territory as the war proceeded.

## Humor in *The Civil War*

Another quality distinguishing *The Civil War* as Southern is humor, which, in its recognizably Southern forms, is often involved with the appreciation of place. We find it, for example, in the Fredericksburg section. Foote remarks that not even among the scenes of carnage at Fredericksburg "did the irrepressible rebel soldier's wry sense of humor—or anyhow what passed for such; mainly it was a biting sense of the ridiculous—desert him" (2:43). And Foote goes on to develop the comment with instances.

Part of the basis on which it is claimed that there is such a thing as a specifically Southern sense of humor, which Shelby Foote himself undoubtedly posesses, often expresses in the narrative, and relishes in historical figures, has been stated by Miss Welty. Her point is that "in humor place becomes its most revealing and at the same time is itself the most revealed . . . because humor . . . of all forms of fiction, entirely accepts place for what it is."[40] She would allow, we believe, an extension of her idea to history—surely humor as a form of history is a pleasant idea. Place is people (and the other way around), and to dwell upon the quiddities of place is to bring out those of personality, humor often arising from recognition of their sheer intransigence.

An illustration of Miss Welty's observation from *The Civil War* is Foote's account of the United States Navy's campaign in his native region, the Yazoo-Mississippi Delta. He rises to sustained comedy in rendering the Yankees' stunned encounter with that intractable place, its incredible climate, jungle, impossible geography, and all that it had bred in the way of varmints and unreconstructible men, black and white. Attempting to take Vicksburg from the land side, the Union navy sent gunboats through the meandering streams of the swampy Delta from the northern end. This exotic expedition had an air of the improbable from the first since it was the fifth in a series—seven attempts were ultimately required—of increasingly frustrating approaches which the Union forces made to Vicksburg.

Undeterred by utter failure of the venture from the north, the Union navy tried again from the south by sending ships in through the mouth of the Yazoo. They steamed into a nightmare of narrow crooked channels overhung with primal cypress and oak in which creatures had taken refuge from flood waters "so that when one of the gunboats struck a tree the quivering limbs let fall a plague of rats, mice, cockroaches, snakes, and lizards" and sometimes coons and wildcats onto the decks (2:208). In the meantime, rebel snipers were at large along the banks, wherever there were any. The expedition ended in ridiculous ignominy, of which even the admiral in command appreciated the humor. It is then part of the effect Foote achieves that he appreciates the wryness of the admiral's memoirs upon which in part he bases his narrative.

A Southern relish for the humorous or absurd aspects of the situations narrated has dictated the choice of much of the matter and colored much more. Although epic in magnitude, seriousness, and scope and tragic in impact, *The Civil War* conveys much of the human quality of events through humor. Foote appreciates, as we have indicated, and features Confederate humor, shares it, and develops it by the special touches of the literary artist. Whether there was actually less humor on the Union side, we cannot say; where it is to be had, as in Lincoln, he shows impartial pleasure in rendering it.

In spite of destruction, carnage, and pain, unforgettably rendered, as in his account of Sharpsburg, Foote will find a place for the humorous touch if any occurred. Here, in an unrelentingly taut episode, the Union general Burnside again figures, duly tagged with his Homeric epithet as "the ruff-whiskered general." We see him watching the bridge over the Antietam "with a fascination amounting to downright prescience, as if he knew already that it was to bear his name and be in fact his chief monument, no matter what ornate shafts of marble or bronze a grateful nation might raise elsewhere in his honor." Rebel guns denied his troops use of the bridge, but he was so "intent on effecting a dry-shod crossing" that it never occurred to him to test the water. "If he had, he would have discovered that the little copper-colored stream, less than fifty feet in width, could have been waded at almost any point without wetting the armpits of the shortest man in his corps" (1:696).

There can be only a touch of it in some passages, but Foote often blends humor into whole sections. That devoted to the Red River campaign in central Louisiana, with its scenes of Union ships caught in shallows above the rapids at Alexandria and being taught by a clever engineering officer to lurch back downstream like disoriented salmon, is as richly amusing as the tales of the Yazoo. The section about "the fiasco " of "an operation that came to be called 'The Crater'"—in which Burnside, as usual appealing to Foote's risibilities, mined and blew up a Confederate fort with an unheard-of quantity of explosives—is laced with humor of "mismanagement at or near the top" and Rube Goldberg ingenuity. The humor enriches and gives hysterical edge to the presentation of an incident which Foote uses as a forward allusion to the better managed explosion at Hiroshima and as a symbol of the lasting effects of the new industrialized warfare: The Crater, he says, "in time would green over and lose its jagged look, but would never really heal" (3:531, 538).

Humor glints in the development of many personages, for example, the sloppy fanatical Stonewall Jackson and his tatterdemalion men when they were doing their exploits against Union troops overpaid, overfed, possibly oversexed, and in any case "down here." He cites the reaction of a Northern reporter wounded near Harpers Ferry and captured who, on learning that the redoubtable Jackson was passing, asked to be raised from his stretcher, took one look, and cried, "O my God! Lay me down" (1:617). Foote more than once thereafter invites in the reader what he calls the "O-my-God-lay-me-down" reaction to extreme types and situations. Humor pervades the handling of the feisty, as for example Earl Van Dorn, or the political, such as Benjamin F. Butler, or the grandiose, such as Pierre G. T. Beauregard and John Charles Frémont.

Eschewing the novelist's license to render psychological time and the play of memory upon his personages' present-time experience, Foote has nevertheless used his own position in after time to provide perspectives on Civil War events which lend them consequence and meaning. He has repeatedly shifted from the past tense to an anterior perspective as well, writing vividly of a "now" in a present-participial, future-conditional mode which invests events, no matter how often rehearsed by others, with a developmental, contingent aspect. He has further retrieved the problematical aspect of historical events-in-the-making by approaching them from a variety of contemporary points of view in order to revive the forces which played for or against the determinations we take retrospectively for granted as "the facts." These are "made new," as Ezra Pound recommended. Something other, the reader feels as people did at the time, might ensue.

Imbued with the sense of place, the sense of history, the sense of literary tradition, *The Civil War* is most profoundly Southern in projecting the sense of tragedy. This has, of course, been attested to by the major critics of Southern literature as a defining characteristic imposed by Southern history. C. Vann Woodward has declared, "The experience of evil and the experience of tragedy are parts of the Southern heritage that are as difficult to reconcile with the American legend of innocence and social felicity as the experience of poverty and defeat are to reconcile with the legends of abundance and success."[41] Without intending paradox, we suggest that insofar as Foote's vision of the Civil War is Southern by virtue of an artistically managed appreciation of the ironic and the tragic, it transcends the parochial and may prove to be the version for all Americans.

### *The Civil War:* Voice and Tone

Through the encompassing narrator's voice, with its shifts, varying of pace, and adjustments of tone, the voice of Shelby Foote tactfully breaks from time to time. It is Shelby Foote all the way, but control is artfully relaxed on occasion to allow more frankly personal tone. There are two strings to this instrument. The narrator's voice, thus varied, is expressive of Foote at his best, consciously representing the best of Southern culture and sensibility.

The narrator's voice is humane, variously bitter, humorous, ironic, or poetic. The reader is pleased and reassured to hear it for its own sake as well as for what it conveys or chooses to emphasize, without ever suggesting that another writer might not deploy other and equally acceptable emphases. The most frequent sort of candid authorial intervention is the brief aside, usually between dashes, serving to tie the action being narrated to others, to comment, to draw a literary or historical parallel, to provide perspective. More extended authorial interventions come in the form, for example, of judgments or acknowledgments that judgment must remain moot on this or that individual or event.

Repeatedly, the author's voice sounds recognizably at the end of a battle narrative, however excitedly it may have been told, to tot up "the butcher's bill" and compare the appalling totals of casualties increasing from battle to battle as the Civil War turned into "the Thing," that is, industrialized total war. In a chapter headed "War Means Fighting . . ." we are given Shiloh as "the first great modern battle" and the shock of it to even the professional soldiers. Beforehand, the author gives us Albert Sidney Johnston, who had husbanded his meager forces and bluffed as long as he could: "He was faced now with the actual bloody thing" (1:192). Afterward, he gives us Grant, soberly realizing that nothing short of absolute conquest was going to settle matters.

Stemming no doubt from Shelby Foote's predilections as a "serious writer," love of language is everywhere evident both as a quality of the narrator's voice and as a selective factor helping to determine which facts that voice relates or stresses. It would be possible to write a respectable history of the Civil War without featuring the articulateness, so mortifying in contrast to the banal expression of Americans in our own period, of the participants. Foote savors even the overblown rhetoric of some of the nineteenth-century figures though he is quick to deflate it by juxtaposing, for example, General John Pope's grandiloquent dispatches from his "Headquarters in the Saddle" with the private soldiers' "jibe that he had his headquarters where his hindquarters ought to be" (1:529–30).

It was love of language that dictated the development of a minor figure, the Union General Samuel R. Curtis, in a memorable passage in which he is proved a commander of language as well as of men and valuable on both heads in Foote's accounting. Curtis, a homely, unromantic, but uxorious man who loved the natural world and the singing of birds, is presented after the battle of Elkhorn Tavern through and partly for the sake of a letter he wrote to his wife. (We are reminded of Captain Fountain in *Shiloh*.) He "moved his headquarters off a ways" under Pea Ridge, Foote tells us, because of the taint of decay rising from the dead on the field of which he is the victor. Foote writes: "'Silent and sad' were words he used to describe the present scene of recent conflict. 'The vulture and the wolf have now communion, and the dead, friends and foes, sleep in the same lonely grave.' So he wrote, this highly practical and methodical engineer. Looking up at the tree-fledged ridge with its gray outcroppings of granite, he added that he hoped it would serve hereafter as a monument to perpetuate the memory of those who had fallen at its base" (1:293).

This passage illustrates the many controlled "poetic" compositions which enrich *The Civil War,* sometimes using the words of participants, sometimes Foote's own, and often, as above, skillfully blending them. Such passages are often a quick touch only, as when Foote presents Stonewall Jackson's men "following the railroad into the sunrise, blood red at first, then fiery in the broad notch of Thoroughfare Gap." Place—and again the weather, outer often suggesting inner—is frequently the subject of the poetry. Take, for example, the evocation of the summer's day on which the fierce and fatal engagement was fought at Seminary Ridge near Gettysburg. "Lee rose by starlight," we are told—phrasing poetic but factual and echoing and prefiguring many symbolic uses of stars throughout in, for example, chapter titles such as "Stars in Their Courses" (many felt that they fought against Lee in Pennsylvania) and "Lucifer in Starlight" (1:615–16; 2:525).

The reader is kept alive to the beauty of the morning as Foote plays it against the tension between Lee and his subordinates over the wisdom of his orders. The Confederate troops, wanting to cheer Lee but keeping still so as not to alert the enemy, "took off their hats in silent salute"; mounted on Traveller, Lee is presented doubling the line, "the sunlight in his gray hair making a glory about his head" (2:535). How bold this is, particularly in the face of our revisionist mood, what command of language against charges, only to be expected, of sentimentality; for it works. There was truth in the poetry as well as in the butcher's bill soon to be presented by Foote as the most disastrous ever to be placed to Lee's account.

## *The Civil War:* Plotting

As applied to a work of history, the term "plotting," since it is normally used with respect to fiction, must be restricted so as not to imply that "the novelist's license" has been impertinently extended. The obvious should be stressed: the historian may not, on pain of losing that character, create or reschedule events. He is, of course, bound by the facts of the past, not only by the order in which events occurred but by their multiplicity. His problem as a writer (assuming his scholarship is impeccable) is to choose which events to tell, establish logical and not merely chronological connections among those he chooses, and tell them with discrimination so as not to swamp his reader with a nerveless recital of one-thing-after-another.

For Foote as for any writer about the past the basic technique was to establish his own identifiable narrative voice, somewhat paradoxically introducing this into historiography, where the requirements of objectivity might seem to rule it out, having eschewed it in his fiction, where it seems that the novelist's license is not unrestricted, either. He succeeded in doing this believably in *The Civil War* taken by itself, but his work in both fiction and history is so much of a piece fundamentally that anyone who reads all of Foote's work will find the authority and persuasiveness of the narrative voice in *The Civil War* supported by the novels and stories. For in the latter, the reader has seen capacity to control point of view and need not fear that his author, on turning to history and speaking in his own voice, will be helplessly opinionated or garrulous. Having gained the reader's confidence, Foote could lay out a course fetching up, necessarily, at a known conclusion and persuade the reader to enjoy following the course laid out for him.

Foote has avoided the looseness of simple chronicle by shuttling back and forth between component narratives of campaigns East and West, political effects North and South, actions on land and sea, and background developments in government and diplomacy. He takes one forward to a high point of suspense, a deferred or suspended resolution, in one campaign, only to turn and develop more or less simultaneous actions elsewhere to their heights and the eventual conclusions involving mutual influences. There may be a lapse of weeks or months between the several perspectives on a given action, so that the reader, though he knows the outcome, is alive to anxieties felt along the way by participants and observers. A temporal dialectic results which yields progression. Foote manages the transitions with constant regard for the cumulative effect of the whole. A "plot" emerges in which momentum mounts from climax to climax and finally to the scene at Appomattox and a gathering of all the scattered parts.

Feeling the novelist's compulsion to shape his work and give it "solidity," Foote went a further distance beyond the merely chronological. It is illuminating to hear him recall that he considered but in the end rejected the idea, reminiscent of the "episodes" of James Joyce's *Ulysses,* of color-coding battles. Explaining that "when I write it's words and commas and semicolons"—and the remark applies as much to his history as to his fiction—he has said he tries to tie in *words* with persons and events. At one time he thought it might be effective to tag, for example, Gettysburg with gold and dusty blue, Sharpsburg with copper and silver, alluding to details of the scenes such as the wheat at Gettysburg and the coppery hue of the creek at Sharpsburg.[42] He did use another device of this sort in attaching Homeric epithets to persons. We soon know that "the ruff-whiskered general" is Burnside, Frémont is "the Pathfinder," Price is "Old Pap" as Halleck is "Old Brains," and George McClellan "Little Mac," "Our George," or "the Little Napoleon." These tags are some of them historical, some supplied by Foote.

For all its amplitude and concreteness, the narrative is firmly organized into three volumes and each of these into three books, the whole comprising in effect an epic prologue and twenty-four chapters in clear allusion to the *Iliad.* The first chapter of volume 1 is a prologue, and the final section of the last chapter of volume 3 serves as an epilogue. The work comes to about 1.6 million words, an immense production but so perspicuously composed, so skillfully paced that the reader is never bored or sated.

Foote has erected in symbolic proportions the figures of Jefferson Davis and Abraham Lincoln, stationing them at the beginning and end and reverting to them frequently throughout. "All men were to be weighed in this time," the author tells us early on, "and especially these two." Beginning with Davis's farewell speech to the United States Senate on January 21, 1861, the prologue moves to Lincoln's furtive entrance into Washington after election to the presidency. Volume 1, *Fort Sumter to Perryville,* closes with the preparations of Davis, now

President of the Confederate States, for his trip to "the troubled western theater" to rally his people as they began to lose romantic illusions and apprehend the seriousness of the war. Foote follows this with an evocation of "the Lincoln music" in an account of the message to Congress in December 1862, in which the Union heard itself eulogized, jug-jug to Confederate ears, as "the last, best hope of earth" (1:166, 810). We hardly need add that Foote, with his love of language, does all justice to the Lincoln music.

Volume 2, *Fredericksburg to Meridian,* opens with Davis's trip west, which gives Foote occasion to develop his own Western-mindedness, not as a contribution to the sometimes tendentious debate as to the relative importance of Virginia and the rest of the South, but as a presentation of the whole Confederacy and its sense of its own manifest destiny in the Southwest and Latin America. He had memorably struck this note in the first volume with a bravura narrative of Henry H. Sibley's horrendous march on Albuquerque and Santa Fe, which Jefferson Davis, who had been chief mover of the Gadsden Purchase, cheered against the odds.

The second volume closes on a Confederacy not only cut off from fantasies of expansion to the Pacific but severed at the Mississippi River and registering W. T. Sherman's articulation of the ominous doctrine of total war. He had already tested this in the punitive devastation of central Mississippi after the fall of Vicksburg— "to the petulant and persistent secessionists, why, death is mercy. . . . " The whole vast work is brought to a distinct climax in the Cincinnati conference between Grant and Sherman, the former having finally been recognized by Lincoln as the general he had to have to win the war, as they concert the Western and Eastern strategies to bring the conflict to an end by waging it totally. Foote sets the two figures earnestly talking in a Cincinnati hotel room against the chiaroscuro of the Confederates' liquidating their pretensions to wage a Second American Revolution reconstituting the principles of the first. They had been forced to enact conscription sometime back, feeling that they thus sacrificed the classic rights for which they fought to the necessities of "the Thing." Now they must extend it to all white males from seventeen to fifty, and Jefferson Davis mourns the necessity "to grind the seed corn of the nation" (2:939, 956).

The final volume, *Red River to Appomattox,* after moving inexorably with sustained narrative art to the laying down of arms on all fronts, comes to a quiet and thoughtful epilogue, a look into the future. The ghost of the murdered Lincoln is summoned, and Foote employs Lincoln's words to suggest his own motivation in writing Civil War history: "What has occurred in this case must ever recur in similar cases. Human nature will not change. In any future great national trial, compared with the men of this, we shall have as weak and as strong, as silly and as wise, as bad and as good. Let us therefore study the incidents of this, as philosophy to learn wisdom from, and none of them as wrongs to be revenged." Foote, the Southerner, would approve, we suspect, the amendment of this by the addition of a phrase—". . . or as complacencies to be defended." He has used Lincoln's remarks as a gloss upon his epigraph from Ecclesiasticus. He goes on to quote Davis, the worn and hounded survivor, though acknowledging that he "could never match that [Lincoln] music, or perhaps even catch its tone," as he asserts at the end his love of America (3:1060). The reader supplies, "All passion spent."

Within the grand epic design, Foote has been unflaggingly ingenious in weaving, stitching, and binding the parts by recurrent themes and characters meant to function, he has said, like the armature within a sculpture. The most pervasive theme, already alluded to several times, is the one Foote has said comes as near as he gets to a thesis, the redressing of the balance between the East and West theaters. By the organization of the material, signaled in the titles of his three volumes, he has kept the relationship East and West in view. By simply featuring in his titles Perryville, Meridian, and Red River, campaigns in the West of which most people know little, he makes his point.

He develops Western actions as fully as Eastern ones and makes mutual effects clear. For example, he narrates events at "Bull Run [in Virginia] and Wilson's Creek [in Missouri], near opposite ends of the thousand-mile-long fighting line" and takes his opportunities to show the reader how a twitch at either end was felt the length of the line (1:120). He gives added coherence to his book by maintaining in the reader's eye, with the aid of images and numerous maps, the whole of the Confederacy as this becomes one enormous battleground and then is contracted under pressure of Winfield Scott's Anaconda strategy, in time split down the Mississippi, and dismembered as the Sherman-Grant strategy and tactics take over.

A related theme is the changing character of the war, begun, especially by the Confederates, under anachronistic notions about individual honor only to develop into the prototype of mass technological warfare. At First Manassas and repeatedly thereafter in 1861–62, there were exploits by mounted heroes with plumes in their bonnets. Foote does justice to these, often ironically but also with affection, admiration, and tears as he follows, for example, the superbly mounted and plumed Jeb Stuart to his Homeric death scene. He brings us on grimly to Cold Harbor and there gives us a glimpse of Colonel Lawrence Keitt of South Carolina thinking to take his chance for glory by leading a green but dashingly uniformed brigade into the fray. "Long on rank but short on combat experience," Foote comments, "he went into his first attack in the gallant style of 1861, leading the way on a spirited gray charger; only to be killed by the first rattling clatter of semiautomatic fire . . . " (3:284).

Foote makes themes illuminate one another often, again, with ironic effect. It is obvious that in narrating the changes in the character of the war he would have repeated occasion to illuminate another major theme, that of the searches by the two presidents for generals competent to understand modern war and prosecute it effectually. It is less obvious that, in giving thematic prominence to the contrast between Northern plenty and Southern poverty, he should have clarified certain tactical issues faced by the presidents and their generals. There is powerful human interest in repeated scenes of hungry, tattered Confederates falling ravenously upon abandoned Yankee supply dumps and stripping Yankee dead, not in Homeric lust for trophies but to obtain food to eat, shoes for bleeding feet, and guns to fire. Cumulatively, such scenes help the reader to understand in concrete terms that in certain circumstances what Foote called their "philosophy of abundance" was a tactical drawback for the Yankees while the Confederates, traveling necessitously light, arrived at some stunning victories under officers such as Jackson and Nathan Bedford Forrest.

Lincoln's long frustration in getting one general after another to move south of the Potomac was caused in part by the generals' preoccupation with the accumulation and defense of immense commissaries which they believed had to follow the armies. Foote prepares the reader to recognize an important development when he presents U.S. Grant finding in December 1862, after Earl Van Dorn destroyed his quartermaster stores at Holly Springs in northern Mississippi, that he could subsist his troops on the countryside deep in enemy territory. Foote quotes Grant's remark, "This taught me a lesson"—and the reader grasps, before Lincoln can, that in his ability to learn this lesson in the West Grant was proving himself to be the long-sought general-in-chief for the East (2:73).

## *The Civil War:* Characterization

Foote sees the characterization of historical personages ultimately as an exercise of literary art, in which he has said that he believes most professional historians do not attain to proficiency.[43] Implicit in his view is the sophisticated recognition that history is a construction of words and commas and semicolons, the quality of which depends as much upon literary skill as upon scholarship or the marshaling of arguments to support a thesis or render a judgment. Foote is concerned rather to create convincing portraits for the sake of intrinsic human interest, to set characters in situations, and to follow the consequences.

Foote brings historical personages hauntingly alive. Their presence is felt even when off-stage, with the result that they function as ligaments binding and articulating the narrative. As figures appear and reappear, Foote develops them in terms of their initiatives and responses in successive crises and engagements. He never presumes to judge absolutely but is only fascinated to observe men of whom he declares, "It was their good fortune, or else their misery, to belong to a generation in which every individual would be given a chance to discover and expose his worth, down to the final ounce of strength and nerve" (1:164). His discretion is constant. If he evidently admires Forrest or McClellan or dislikes Joseph E. Johnston or Phil Sheridan, the reader must infer the fact from characterization fairly and sympathetically developed until the weight of evidence tells.

As Foote has contended that the historian's greatest offense against "the novelist's canon" is likely to lie in characterization,[44] so "Foote's stated aversion to making interpretations would seem to violate one of the historian's most basic obligations," as James I. Robertson, Jr., has commented. Robertson believes Foote deludes himself and in fact "interpretations abound throughout the text," citing as instances Foote's statements about Braxton Bragg, William T. Sherman, and Joseph E. Johnston. These strike Robertson as "interpretations—not facts."[45] The issue here joined is fundamental but may be resolved through consideration of the genre requirements of narrative (not necessarily fictional) on the one hand and of the expository monograph on the other.

Over against Robertson's concern should be set George Garrett's observation that instead of presenting character all at once as in "the unveiling of a statue" and then "determining to what extent the character conformed to or deviated from the initial judgment" as character is usually treated in "conventional history. . . . Foote used the novelist's means, his own, allowing the individual characters to develop and change in and with action and events." We are given "impressions" rather than "judgments." In *The Civil War,* "characterization is dramatic and dynamic and becomes a source of narrative suspense, thus of forward motion in the whole narrative."[46] If a character impresses the reader as noble or mean, brilliant or incompetent, the reason is not that Foote has sneaked in a judgment but that the reader has drawn a conclusion from the "evidenced" characterization.

In characterizing historical figures, Foote generally uses their own words, supplementing them with those of contemporaries and his own, varying tone and language to suit his man. He may provide a brief background or a glimpse of a postwar career to suggest, at least, the rounding for which he cannot halt his narrative of the war. He uses parallel and contrast, for example in developing the "immovables," McClellan on the Union side and Joseph E. Johnston on the Confederate, or in pitting the rash, mercurial Van Dorn against the stolid Curtis at Elkhorn Tavern.

He enlivens history by exhibiting the interplay of personalities, as in narrating the rise of Grant against the prejudice of his superior, Henry Halleck, or the frustration of Beauregard's Napoleonic strategies by the realism of Jefferson Davis colored by the incompatibility of Creole and Anglo-Saxon. The play of personality is nowhere more effectively used than in the narration of the battle of Nashville. Foote shows us Halleck and Grant prodding the Union commander in the field, "Slow Trot" Thomas, and follows Thomas, who like Kutuzov sometimes fell asleep in councils, on his deliberate way to victory over John Bell Hood. Foote multiplies instances of "single combat," reminiscent of the *Iliad,* sometimes between champions on the same side, as in the encounter between Huger and Longstreet at Seven Pines, or between pre-war friends or enemies now on opposing sides, as when Hood faces his West Point roommate John M. Schofield in the final battles for Middle Tennessee.

Foote touches to life not only figures with pervasive roles who function structurally through long stretches of the narrative but also many whom he brings forward on account of some signal action or speech. Often he accords cameo treatment to men responsible for technological advances, thus heightening the theme of modernizing warfare. An exquisite instance of the cameo is Foote's introducing handsome Major Roberdeau Wheat of Louisiana into the account of First Manassas where, wounded and told by a doctor his wound was mortal, the young man said, "I don't feel like dying yet." The doctor told him, "There is no instance on record of recovery from such a wound." "Well then," replied Wheat, "I will put my case on record." He did so, and Foote notices him again the next spring at New Market and then records his death two months later at Turkey Hill. Again a participant's language has commanded space in the narrative, and the narrative profited. The reader remembers with a pang Roberdeau Wheat putting his case at last on record, and that pang helps discriminate and memorialize these battles as human experience (cf. 1:83, 428, 487).

Foote's most distinguished achievement in handling character in *The Civil War* is his structural use of it. As we have noted, one of Hume's devices in the *History of England* was to introduce character studies of historical personages to vary and add a dimension to chronology. His studies derived in part from the seventeenth-century genre known as "the character." Like his appendices on cultural topics, his "characters" remained distinct from his narrative. He did not develop a technique whereby he could integrate the character studies and use them to unify his material and give it movement. Other historians since have done so with varying success. Among them, Shelby Foote seems to us to have met the highest standard.

He has done this, first, by distributing his treatment of any given character through the narrative and, second, by preserving the developmental quality of each characterization. Any given figure is presented as changing under the impact of successive events, so that his story has its own momentum which, duly subordinated in the narrative of the war, nevertheless helps drive that main "plot." Major figures, appearing and reappearing throughout, have the effect of motifs repeated and varied. Even an incidental character, such as Roberdeau Wheat, has a powering effect and, for as long as his short thread runs, contributes suspense and movement.

To illustrate Foote's technique in characterizing historical persons, we have chosen to discuss his treatment of John Bell Hood, Philip Sheridan, and Nathan Bedford Forrest. They exemplify, respectively, figures toward whom we infer that Foote's own feelings were neutral, negative, and admiring. For there is no doubt that the reader knows whom the author likes or dislikes. In a television interview, Dick Cavett raised this issue. Foote candidly acknowledged the circumstance but remarked that the matter reduces to technique which, backed by inclusive sympathy, develops and reveals qualities both good and evil without the necessity of authorial judgments.

Foote brings a figure onstage at a point where the war narrative requires him but usually manages to do so with a characteristic speech or action which starts the duly subordinated development. Hood enters in the spring of 1862. McClellan has landed troops in the Virginia Peninsula from transports in the James River and is threatening Richmond. Hood, commanding Texas and Georgia troops, is under the command of Joseph E. Johnston, who has ordered an attack but does not wish to start a general engagement. The Federals are "hit harder than Johnston intended," and he admonishes "the blond-bearded six-foot-two-inch Kentucky brigadier: 'General Hood, have you given an illustration of the Texas idea of feeling an enemy gently and falling back? What would your Texans have done, sir, if I had ordered them to charge and drive back the enemy?' Hood's blue eyes were somber. He said gravely, 'I suppose, General, they would have driven them into the river, and tried to swim out and capture the gunboats'" (1:412).

Within the fifteen lines used to introduce Hood, only incidentally to the narrative of the Peninsula campaign, the reader learns that he is thirty years of age, a West Pointer, native of Kentucky, who had served under Albert Sidney Johnston before the war, now commanding a Texas and Georgia brigade. His appearance is sketched, his impetuosity suggested. Moreover, the characterization of Johnston, famous or infamous for his Fabian tactics, is advanced, as is the larger theme of the conflict of personalities among the Confederate generals which was one of Lee's main problems. These two will have their run-ins in the future.

Foote then provides an incremental presentation extending to near the end of the narrative. He shows Hood through his men's enthusiastic responses, his interaction—often stormy—with military peers and superiors, and the reactions of society women in Columbia and Richmond who lionize him and follow his star-crossed love affair with a

South Carolina belle. Foote shows him also at the height of the action at numerous engagements, receiving wounds—the maiming of an arm, the loss of a leg—but returning fierily to the field. By the time Hood is assigned command of the Army of Tennessee in the desperate time of Joseph E. Johnston's dismissal on the outskirts of Atlanta, Foote has provided so many views that the reader understands, without being told, why Hood was finally the choice of the Confederate leaders and equally why it was a choice against all but decisive doubts about him.

A cerain flatness is imposed upon the characterization by the necessity of subordinating it to the main narrative, but Foote suggests roundness even though he cannot fully develop it. Hood is mainly the reckless blond giant whose aggressiveness could be counted on in a pinch although his prudence and grasp of the long view might be in doubt. He was ambivalent about his promotion to commander of the Army of Tennessee, and Foote affectingly renders his agony of self-knowledge so that we are the more impressed—and alarmed—by Hood's ability to reassert his aggressiveness, reinvigorate his demoralized army, and attempt to return to the enemy's frontiers in the Lee-Jackson style of 1862. When he has led his army to fearful destruction at Franklin and Nashville, Foote is unsparing in assessing responsibility yet still presents Hood in all the ambiguity of his character and in the light of all the long narrative of the war. He failed, but the threat he mounted was real to the last, as Foote makes us realize by quoting the alarmed communications from Washington to Hood's opponent, Thomas.

The portrait of Philip H. Sheridan which emerges from Foote's pages in some ways parallels that of Hood as well as that of Forrest, all three being general officers noted for aggressiveness. Sheridan is introduced rather formally with two paragraphs of background, physical description, and statement about personality. These are placed in the account of the Perryville campaign where, only two weeks after becoming a brigadier, the thirty-one-year-old Ohioan more than justified his promotion and began to make a name with the public (see 1:732–38).

We learn that Sheridan is the son of Irish immigrants and brings to the war hatred for the South grounded in class animosity. This stems from an encounter with a scion of Virginia aristocracy at West Point. His ruthlessness as a commander is further explained by his love of the limelight and extreme ambition. He denied what others believed—that he was born either in Ireland or en route to the United States, "not only because he was strenuously American and preferred to think of himself as having sprung from native soil, but also because he learned in time that no person who drew his first breath outside its limits could ever become President of the United States." He is five feet five inches tall, "bandy-legged . . . with heavy, crescent-shaped eyebrows, cropped hair, and a head as round as a pot" and "looked more like a Mongolian than like the Irishman he was." This is Little Phil, "a man in a hurry" (1:732).

Along the way, we gain plentiful insight into Sheridan's "instinct for aggression," as Foote puts it, and learn by the by that his idea of an Indian policy for the West was genocide. When Grant summoned him to Virginia, Sheridan "brought something different and hard into the army he now joined." His tone is summed up in his exclamation, "Smash 'em up! Smash 'em up!" The reader does not doubt that this was the man for the job when Grant decided to apply in the Shenandoah Valley the scorched-earth policy Sherman perfected in Mississippi and Georgia. The devastation of the Valley under Sheridan's direction was complete: "To hurt the people the land itself was hurt . . . " (2:721; 3:135–36, 564).

The characterization of Sheridan will leave the reader persuaded of something inimical in this man while Foote's treatment of the closest Confederate parallel, Nathan Bedford Forrest, has a very different effect. Both gained reputation as cavalry commanders capable of improbable exploits in and around and behind enemy lines which make for rousing narrative, but there is a difference illustrated by Sheridan's "Smash 'em up!" compared with Forrest's motif, "Charge! Charge!" In portraying Forrest, as well as Robert E. Lee, a Southern writer may be suspected of feeling the pull of ancestral piety leading to bias in characterization. It is also the case that, if Forrest has been a cult figure in the South, he has hardly been forgiven elsewhere for his pre-war career as a slave dealer and his post-war activity in the Ku Klux Klan. For these reasons it seems advisable to look for an answer to the question: is there justification for Foote's leaving the reader with a negative feeling about the Major General of Cavalry, U.S.A., but with admiration for the Major General of Cavalry, C.S.A.?

There is no more doubt in *The Civil War* than in *Shiloh* about the author's view, and the issue is only whether the evidence supports it. Foote introduces Forrest as a lieutenant colonel, forty years of age, with little formal schooling and no military education, when he has just executed at Bowling Green classic cavalry maneuvers "which he could not identify by name and of which he had most likely never heard." He personally killed one enemy officer by shooting, another by sabering, and dislocated the shoulder of a third. He is described "standing in the stirrups, swinging his sword, and roaring, 'Charge! Charge!'" (1:171–72). Foote will be at pains to bring out in narratives later on an element only implicit here. When Forrest roared "Charge!" his men responded. The point is made again and again that he knew how to set an example and shape raw recruits very quickly into effectual soldiers. His quality as a leader in the field reflected real capacity as strategist and tactician, and his men trusted him.

By the summer of 1862, Forrest had recovered from the wound he suffered at Shiloh. He had submitted to surgery without anesthesia in the field for removal of a ball from his spine, and "recovery" must have been a very relative term. Grievously wounded in April, he was in action again by June. For operations against Grant's rail supply lines in Middle Tennessee, Forrest molded 2,100 troopers "mostly recruits newly brigaded under his command and mainly armed with shotguns and flintlock muskets" into a force which in three weeks time became another matter altogether. The recruits achieved all the strategic objectives assigned to them and in the process found themselves transformed into veterans outfitted with horses, weapons, and supplies taken from the enemy (2:65–69).

Foote dramatizes Forrest's hold on his men with an account of an episode during these forays in Middle Tennessee. Pursued by three Union brigades in the closing days of December 1862, Forrest was in a tight place between Huntingdon and Clarksburg. He had begun negotiating the unconditional surrender of one of the Union brigades after a four-hour artillery duel when he was attacked from the rear. "For the first last only time in his career, Forrest was completely surprised in battle. . . . resuming the fight to his front, he simultaneously charged rearward, stalling the surprise attackers with blows to the head and flanks, and withdrew sideways before his opponents recovered from the shock." Summing up all that Forrest accomplished in these actions, Foote ends with the effect on Forrest's men: "They saw all this as Forrest's doing, and it was their pride, now and for all the rest of their lives—whether those lives were to end next week in combat or were to stretch on down the years to the ones they spent sunning their old bones on the galleries of crossroads stores throughout the Deep and Central South—that they had belonged to what in time would be known as his Old Brigade" (2:68, 69).

But Forrest had defects, and Foote is not blind to them. He was often at odds with his more orthodox superiors. Jefferson Davis acknowledged to Forrest after the war, when he paid him a deathbed visit and then attended his funeral, that the Richmond authorities had been slow to understand and appreciate his innovations. Forrest could be brutally insubordinate, as when he came to defy Braxton Bragg after the battles around Chattanooga in 1863. He insulted Bragg outrageously and predicted to a companion that Bragg would do nothing, imputing cowardice. George Garrett has praised Foote for the way in which he treats this incident involving a highly unsympathetic figure, Bragg, and Forrest, who "has long since been established as one of the narrative's genuine heroes." Foote intervenes to make clear that Bragg, whatever his faults, was no coward and had properly overriding motives in overlooking Forrest's misconduct. "We learn," Garrett says, "two things from the brief episode, some sense of the limits of Forrest's imagination, intelligence, and judgment, and some awareness of strengths in Bragg's flawed character."[47]

Foote's treatment of Forrest, while it should be appreciated as prose responding in virtuoso fashion to splendid material, should also be considered in the light of a statement Foote has made in various contexts that in his opinion the two geniuses developed during the war were Abraham Lincoln and Nathan Bedford Forrest. He sees them both as almost evolutionary adaptations to "the Thing," Lincoln learning on the job how to orchestrate industrialized warfare, Forrest how to respond from the weaker side with guerrilla and partisan strategy and tactics. Foote reminds the reader that what Forrest did, at Brices's Crossroads for instance, is still studied in the war colleges and has gained new relevance since the war in Vietnam. The two figures are not commensurate, and Foote does not suggest they are. He does, however, dignify Forrest as a natural genius in his more limited sphere, and with more respectable motivation than his Union counterpart, Sheridan.

Shelby Foote exhibits in *The Civil War* undeviating interest in human character and appetite for human experience. He knows that there is always a mixture of qualities in men, that heroism is not exclusive. There *are* heroes here, however, North and South, no matter how ironic Foote's view may be in general. There is magnanimity for the men who break or fail, such as Hood or the Union General William S. Rosecrans, who abandoned the field at Chickamauga; for the tests they had to meet are rendered in all their formidableness. Some persons of the drama emerge as distinctly villainous, such as Edwin M. Stanton, through scrupulously sympathetic presentation. The author almost entirely exludes the judgmental or even the argumentative tone.

We think it probable that the passion which powers *The Civil War,* informs the narrative with novelistic life, and makes it history rather than analysis or essay is Foote's fascination with men of all kinds as they were proved in memorable scenes. He is something more and other than the expert sportscaster, excitedly guiding the reader and enhancing his appreciation of a complex sequence of actions, to whom Gallie compares the historian in one of his functions. He is an aficionado, not necessarily of war, but of the testing of men under extreme pressure; for he has faith that some, at least, will rise to the occasion and set a standard while others, if they fail, earn understanding and pity. Although on reflection he may be appalled, Foote pays steady attention to the organized carnage, feels in it ritualistic value, and conveys the supra-sexual male transport of battle as ritual played out to actual death. This is the fuel of the narrative vigor of his hour-by-hour rendering, for example, of the terrible suicidal scenes at Gettysburg or Cold Harbor. And it is vigor generated in such scenes which, throttled by considerations of art, guarantees the steady pace of the dominant narrative voice, through which the author's personal tones, humane, ironic, sometimes freely excited, break with effect also artistic.

## Chapter Seven

# Returning to Jordan County

The tripartite structures that Shelby Foote has so often favored in his works are clearly reflected in his career. He closed the first phase, devoted to fictional narratives, with *Jordan County* in 1954. The second phase, extending through twenty years, was devoted to the three volumes of *The Civil War*. In the midst of his preoccupation with narrative history, he reprinted in 1964, in a one-volume edition entitled *Three Novels,* the Jordan County fiction he was most concerned to preserve as an earnest of his intention to resume novel-writing. Faithful to his program, he began the third phase of his career in 1976 with the writing of a novel about Jordan County types set, however, in Memphis, entitled *September September* and published in 1978. He is now writing a novel which takes him home again since it is a further development of the Jordan County "landscape in narrative" with which he began.

He has stated that his first five novels "made a unit, a definite stage." By no means finished with the Jordan County subject matter, he nevertheless felt a need for technical innovation in his handling of it. "But apparently I was not ready to move on to another style of novel at that point," he continued. "So I turned to history, which in my handling of it, is another style of novel. . . . "[1] In the historical novel *Shiloh,* he had a point of departure for the long excursion into nonfictional narrative on which we have followed him.

George Garrett observed in an assessment of *The Civil War* following publication of the final volume that it had become possible to "see some general things" about Foote's early novels "more clearly" in the light of his application of the novelist's technique to history. Garrett correctly predicted that the novels would "have a kind of second life." With the exception of *Tournament,* they are all being reprinted and widely translated. A new generation of readers is in a position to test Garrett's judgment that the novels have not dated and "are, therefore, not to be taken as exemplary of any particular school or movement or, for that matter, any single *period*. They are highly individual, independent works."²

The achievement of individuality and independence proved above all that in his first phase Foote had assimilated to his own autonomous art the given and inescapable influence of William Faulkner. The point should be stressed, for Foote's novels are still sometimes derogated as derivative. An early instance was the reviewer for the *Times Literary Supplement* who said that *Follow Me Down* is written "in a style much indebted to Mr. William Faulkner," an observation as cavalier as the same reviewer's statement that the novel is set "in the American Middle West."³ We have enumerated the distinctions of Foote's work in this regard and add as confirmation Garrett's assertion, "it is clear that Foote was not influenced [by Faulkner] in any of the obvious and negative ways." He credits Foote with a prose style readily distinguishable from Faulkner's, "characterized by a kind of classic clarity and condensation, often transparent, though the *materials* he deals with may be complex and dark."⁴

The importance of discriminating Foote's work from Faulkner's has been pointed up by Walter Sullivan's warning that "one is likely to be fooled into believing that Foote's work is cast absolutely in the old mold." Taking *Follow Me Down* as characteristic, he marks the ways in which it differs from novels by Faulkner. Its chief distinguishing aspects are "the tightness of its structure" and Foote's explicitness about its "philosophical foundation" upon "the Biblical standard . . . a system older and better-established than any Southern code. . . ."⁵

To which should be added a further comment by Garrett that in characterization Foote uses "a method of continuing *development*" contrasting with Faulkner's "characterization by discovery." Like Faulkner, Foote has adopted a "basic pattern, a combination of structure and point of view . . . different for each story," but unlike Faulkner "he neither invents new forms for story-telling, nor in any of his work is the means or strategy anything more (or less) than a precision tool for his overall purpose." Although Foote's stories, like Faulkner's, are "rooted in history," it is history of Foote's place not Faulkner's.⁶

Through the first four of the five novels from the early phase we have noted increasing authority and ingenuity in a certain kind of narrative patterning, but for the fifth Foote made a marked change which may hint something as to the different "style of novel" he hankered for. Everything up to *Jordan County,* and indeed the component stories in that book of uncertain genre, was tightly and economically structured, written to the order of preconceived outlines. In that sense, the first four novels were "safe," like the musical compositions of Harry Van in "Ride Out" before he heard Duff Conway's jazz improvisations. Did Shelby Foote begin to dare less control and more feeling, to take the risks of technique at the command of expression and not the other way around?

At all events, *Jordan County* is looser, with discontinuities, uneven development of parts, and comparative uncertainty of ultimate effect, than anything before it. Yet in several characters, notably Duff Conway and Isaac Jameson—and in a third, less successful, in our opinion, but also close to the author's feelings, Hector Wingate Sturgis of "Child by Fever"—*Jordan County* proves itself upon the reader's pulses. Except for Hugh Bart of *Tournament,* where the final effect is ambivalent, no other characters in the canon seem so distinctly plugged into the current of the author's emotion although his sympathies have accommodated, for example, Luther Eustis of *Follow Me Down.*

*The Civil War,* developing out of its overture, *Shiloh,* a cycle of monologues planned in advance, paradoxically proved a broad channel for emotion while requiring the discipline of research and minute application of technique on the grandest scale. We are tempted to assert that Foote's major achievement in this work of history is the superb craftsmanship displayed in organization and articulation of masses of material. As he was finishing the work, he said in an interview, "I'm working with a very large canvas, but at the same time I'm trying to do each paragraph the way you'd write a sonnet. I'm trying for precision on a large scale."[7] What he tried to do, he did, but tried for much more than precision and perspicuity.

For, as our account of it has gone to show, *The Civil War* is intended as an epic—"my iliad," the author calls it—and is rich with feeling for the fathers of the nation, North and South. We believe that the source of the feeling which brings life to history can be located in the fiction, where it has, however, not yet flowed so freely and copiously. Shelby Foote has needed, as man and writer, to find and, if he cannot repair, to comprehend in his art a connection to father and grandfather and great-grandfather. In fiction, he has come nearest to doing this in the characters of Isaac Jameson of "Pillar of Fire" and Hugh Bart of *Tournament.* Yet in the fiction his artist types—Duff Conway, Hector Wingate Sturgis—come to no good end. We call it remarkable, therefore, that Shelby Foote the artist, speaking in his own voice in *The Civil War,* was at last able to do ample justice by the crucial generation, including its Delta representatives.

Everything he learned about writing novels in the first phase proved transferable to writing history. It appears that the discipline of research, consideration of all aspects of a large public event, and increased appreciation of human capacities are carrying over from the experience of producing *The Civil War* into the fiction Foote now writes. Setting himself an exercise to prepare his return to the Matter of Jordan County, he wrote what he somewhat deprecatingly calls his "action novel," *September September.* We recall, however, that he never felt apologies necessary for writing "action history"—military hitory focused upon the "face of battle." This most recent novel also uses action in the service of serious purpose: again, as in *The Civil War,* the fundamental concern is to render human character as it develops under extreme testing.

### *September September*

Foote has commented in conversation with us that he wished to try his hand at treating "black bourgeois characters and the problem of their imitation of whites," and it is the black family Kinship of Memphis, but with connections to Bristol and Jordan County, which proves its mettle in *September September.* The Kinships' ordeal occurs during September 1957. In conscious extension of the research methods he had brought to expertness in producing history, Foote imbued himself with the details of that short period. He intended not so much to incorporate information in the novel as to refresh his memory of events he himself had experienced as crucial at the time and to write as if still within the chosen ambience. Of course, details of the time surface in the narrative; but this is not so "safe" as to rely upon a literal day-by-day recital.

He chose September 1957 for several reasons, some directly functional with respect to his plot, some of symbolic value only generally relevant to his characters and their situation. Among the latter is the circumstance that Ford's unfortunate Edsel automobile was

introduced that month and appears briefly in the novel as an indication
that things might go amiss on the American scene. The month had
barely passed when, on October 4, "the Russians put the sputnik up
from Kazakhstan, a polished steel basketball with spike antennas,
beeping in A-flat around and around a world that would never be the
same" (289).[8] It was part of the ambience out of which the novel was
written, though not spelled out in it, that Foote was powerfully affected
by this event. He has said that "it destroyed a basic belief" that he,
growing up in the 1920s and 1930s, shared with many of his
generation—faith in science, thought to be necessarily and exclusively
the province of free men. The Russians and their captured German
scientists proved it not so, and Foote says he saw the sputnik episode "as
the exact lip of an enormous crater that yawned [one recalls The Crater
near Petersburg in volume 3 of *The Civil War*], and now we are
separated by that date."[9]

The public event which most intimately affects the novel was
President Eisenhower's ordering troops to Little Rock, Arkansas, to
enforce racial integration of Central High School. The Arkansas capital
is 135 miles west of Memphis, which reacted with considerable tense-
ness. Foote posits three criminally inclined Jordan County characters
who see in the situation an opportunity to kidnap a little black boy,
Teddy Kinship, grandson of Theo G. Wiggins, a wealthy and powerful
figure. Their idea is that in the racially polarized city a black family can
be persuaded not to call in the white police and will, therefore, pay a
ransom. Foote adds "a nice bit of counterpoint" to remind readers that
bigotry was not the monopoly of any one section: one of the kidnappers
comments satirically on a news story about the banning that month by
the New York Board of Education of *Huckleberry Finn* on account of its
bearing on race relations.[10]

The Memphis scene in September 1957 is circumstantially rendered
but only incidentally to the action. The accurate presentation of parts of
the city and its mores at that time of social change serves structural
purposes. There are brief but thoughtfully disposed glimpses into the
recent past—of Mr. Crump, W. C. Handy, and life on Beale Street—
and allusions to traditional practices, only now coming into question,
of racial discrimination. Yellow Cabs are reserved for whites, the
Mid-South Fair sets aside one day for the admission of blacks, there is a
matter-of-fact reference to "the law [that] is first of all the white man's

law" (146). Foote is accurate whenever he has occasion in the narrative to mention the weather, street names, restaurants, prices, movies, and television programs.

The Jordan County characters are Podjo, a gambler who has served time at Parchman, the Mississippi prison farm, for manslaughter committed during a fracas over a married woman; the woman Reeny; and her current attachment Rufus, also an ex-convict and a drifter. These three have complex Jordan County antecedents, not much developed but meaningful to anyone who has read Foote's other fiction. Podjo, son of a tough logger and a religious Sicilian woman, earned the Silver Star under Patton; but what he values from World War II is skill acquired in gambling, of which he has made a career. We recall Hugh Bart from *Tournament,* Harley Drew from *Love in a Dry Season.* Nevertheless, Podjo is the steady, cautious member of the party, determined to avoid violence.

Reeny shares with Podjo a southern Jordan County background— they will know where Solitaire is. She undoubtedly knows the Eustis family, being the daughter of Brother Jimson, the "loud and strong" preacher in *Follow Me Down.* She and Podjo, six years her elder, were schoolchildren in Ithaca and may conceivably have been taught by Miss Bertha Tarfeller. Thirty-five and conscious of age, Reeny, widow of a Marine killed on Guadalcanal, has had various liaisons and now is combination mother and lover of Rufus Hutton, eight years her junior. During the action, she transfers her maternal feelings to the little boy they kidnap and proves kindhearted and likable in other ways as well. Like Podjo, to whom she transfers the other component of her affections, she wants no violence beyond the mimimum necessary in "snatching" the child.

Rufus Hutton is a Bristol boy who has gone even further astray than his country-bred companions. He is the grandson of Mr. Cilley, bookkeeper in Lawrence Tilden's bank *(Love in a Dry Season).* He has spent two years at Ole Miss, but such education as he acquired has served only to heighten his illusions. A reviewer discussed him as an instance in current fiction of characters "whose dreams and schemes all derive from movie and television illusions."[11] A handsome man, he is also a compulsive liar, infantile, totally unpredictable and unreliable. His partners in crime find him out but not soon enough to prevent his ruining their "caper."

Eben Kinship, the major Negro character, also has a Jordan County background; his quarrelsome parents had a café in Bristol. His sister Julia precipitates Duff Conway's killing his rival in "Ride Out." Handsome, dignified, and responsible, though evidently constrained by respectability naively modeled on the white middle class, Eben also served in World War II. He acquired some education and lives in Memphis with his wife Martha and their children, a girl of six and a boy of eight. The Kinships live near Martha's father, Theo G. Wiggins, for whom Eben works. Wiggins dominates Eben and his family, and all of them live as well as they can within the oppressive white-dominated structure of Memphis not yet shaken by the civil rights movement.

The action moves quickly and steadily, and suspense is maintained through the last paragraph. With even attention to both black and white characters, Foote sketches the backgrounds together with the planning of the crime. Eben's son Teddy is kidnapped and kept in the attic of a house on the bluff over the Mississippi River—a neighborhood where Foote lived briefly, now obliterated by urban renewal. The child is eventually returned unharmed, and a complex aftermath ensues.

The destinies of all of the characters take decisive turns. Rufus meets the violent death he has long courted. Podjo and Reeny go off to further adventures. The character most fundamentally affected is Eben Kinship, who, in the course of his ordeal, defines his manhood against his strong-willed father-in-law. As a result, Eben assumes for the first time a proper posture in his relationship with his wife Martha. During ten years of marriage, she has really been wedded to somewhat distorted and anachronistic ideas of white gentility and looked to her father rather than her husband. In sympathetically broaching the predicament of the black bourgeoisie in combining mature self-respect with the necessity of looking to white manners for a standard, Foote entered a region of American experience which has not yet been thoroughly explored in fiction.

All of the characters are individualized, discriminated by speech patterns, language, and mannerisms. The interwoven themes combine the topical with the permanent—when social content is sifted out, and sifted it must be, it is weighty. Foote turns stereotypes upside down, for example in contrasting Martha Kinship, straitlaced, inhibited, but made more human by her testing, with Reeny, morally loose and taking life as it comes. One of the most memorable characters, bearing thematic weight and alluding to figures in the history of Memphis, is

Theo G. Wiggins. He learned how to live and prosper in the city dominated by the Crump machine, "using their own system to beat them with." Nevertheless, he realizes that his way is "going fast," that his son-in-law will live in his own way, and that the world of his beloved grandson will be different—perhaps even better (289).

*September September* is distinguished, like all of Foote's work, by skillful handling of narrative point of view. Four omniscient sections frame and alternate with three sections called "Voices": Podjo, Eben, Rufus; then Reeny, Martha, Reeny again; finally Rufus, Eben, and Podjo: the women framed by the men, the blacks by the whites. These first-person parts provide intimate access to characters and motives, variety of style and tone, and not a little of the humor and irony that pervade the novel. The crime has unexpected results, some beneficent. The cool, level tone of the omniscient narrator's parts does not allow anything so rash as a happy-ever-after conclusion, but the Kinships are happier. There is no doubt that the two surviving villains will go on together; they, like the sputnik, are "in orbit."

## Work in Progress

Since publishing *September September,* Foote has been at work on a major novel of Jordan County. Beyond a few general statements, he does not discuss work in progress. Of the new novel, he has said that it will be entitled "Two Gates to the City," which he began outlining twenty-five years ago. He has referred to it as "a Mississippi Karamazov," from which we infer that it will be comprehensive and massive, on the grand theme of fathers and children under the Delta dispensation. It will deal with "a struggle for values in the modern South."[12] Making it clear that his plan may change and that he himself has changed through the years, he has indicated that the novel will be set in Bristol "in the late 40s and on through to the mid-60s." It will be "about three cousins and their grandfather . . . a family novel" though not a "saga."[13]

Those who are familiar with all Foote's works will be intrigued to learn that the central characters of "Two Gates to the City" are descendants of the Yankee lieutenant who participated in the burning of the original mansion on Solitaire during the Civil War, as narrated in "Pillar of Fire." This story, though scarcely the length of a novella, is at the heart of the Matter of Jordan County. Lieutenant Lundy, given very mixed feelings about the destruction of the house, the death of the pioneer Isaac Jameson during the process, and the ethical aspects of the burning expedition, evidently returns to the scene after the Civil War—very distinctly the outsider Foote has repeatedly introduced into his Delta landscape. He could obviously function as a nexus into which all the strands of Foote's work could be gathered and from which his modern developments could derive.

Now well into the third phase of his career, Shelby Foote, committed first and last to the novel, faces with assurance what must nevertheless seem at times an overwhelming question: whether he can match in the novel the mark he has set in history. He seems determined to "ride out" in the novel with "Two Gates to the City." Not that we predict truncation of his career, as allusion to Duff Conway might suggest. Still other fictions may of course follow, but he has more than once said that for him the assassination of President Kennedy seems to make a reasonable end to the period he wishes to compass. "Two Gates to the City" will apparently extend to that point.

Philippe Jaworski, an able French commentator on Foote, has made an observation about the seven narratives in *Jordan County* which applies as well to all Foote's works, namely, that they raise the question "of the nature of historical discourse: it is a matter of knowing how to *tell* History." He asserts that in the novella "Child by Fever" Foote demonstrated "a true interrelationship between the deciphering of History and a narrative in which the narrator will be at the same time ouside of the narrative content and capable of exploring the secret of its depths." Jaworski credits Foote, in short, with having developed "the *novelistic* formula, candidly and deliberately novelistic, which alone can know nothing yet know everything, be ignorant of all yet tell all, lie yet speak true."[14]

Not yet having fully taken the measure of *The Civil War,* Foote's French commentators probably do not entirely appreciate the grandeur of his ambition—if we read him correctly—to compete in fiction with his own work in history. They comprehend, however, more thoroughly than his American critics seem to have done "the logic and the privilege of novelistic art" which he exemplifies.[15] But he looks now to a transcendent dimension of his art where everything is to be under control yet totally expressive.

# Notes and References

*Chapter One*

1. Elmo Howell, "The Greenville Writers and the Mississippi Country People," *Louisiana Studies* 8 (Winter 1969):348.
2. Ibid.
3. Eudora Welty, *Delta Wedding* (New York: Harcourt, Brace & World, 1946), p. 4.
4. Ibid., pp. 4–5.
5. John Carr, "It's Worth a Grown Man's Time: Shelby Foote," in *Kite-Flying and Other Irrational Acts: Conversations with Twelve Southerners,* ed. John Carr (Baton Rouge: Louisiana State University Press, 1972), p. 20.
6. William Faulkner, *Go Down, Moses,* The Modern Library (New York: Random House, 1942), p. 335.
7. Ibid.
8. Ibid., p. 340.
9. Carr, p. 20.
10. Faulkner, p. 364.
11. Carr, p. 20.
12. Faulkner, p. 364.
13. William Faulkner, "Mississippi," *Holiday,* April 1954, p. 38.
14. *Encyclopaedia Britannica,* 15th ed., s.v. "Mississippi," by John N. Burrus.
15. See Redding S. Sugg, Jr., "John's Yoknapatawpha," *South Atlantic Quarterly* 68 (Summer 1969):348–49.
16. William Alexander Percy, *Lanterns on the Levee: Recollections of a Planter's Son* (New York: Alfred A. Knopf, 1941), pp. 3, 4.
17. Richard H. King, *A Southern Renaissance: The Cultural Awakening of the American South, 1930–1955* (New York: Oxford University Press, 1980), pp. 85–86.
18. Percy, p. 153.
19. Ibid., p. 345.
20. Ibid., p. 19.
21. Howell, p. 354.
22. David L. Cohn, *Where I Was Born and Raised* (Boston: Houghton Mifflin Co., 1948), p. 27.
23. Ibid., pp. 25, 27–28.

24. Hodding Carter, *Where Main Street Meets the River* (New York: Rinehart & Co., 1952), p. 70.

25. Howell, p. 352.

26. Redding S. Sugg, Jr., "Hodding Carter: Southern Legacy," *Atlanta,* November 1969, p. 53.

27. Thomas BeVier, "Pericles, Pride and Greenville," *Memphis Commercial Appeal Mid-South Magazine,* 14 July 1968, p. 4.

28. Shelby Foote, "Faulkner's Depiction of the Planter Aristocracy," in *The South and Faulkner's Yoknapatawpha: The Actual and the Apocryphal,* ed. Evans Harrington and Ann J. Abadie (Jackson: University Press of Mississippi, 1977), pp. 40–41.

29. Ibid., p. 49.

30. Ibid.

31. Ibid., p. 48.

32. Carr, pp. 22–23.

33. We are indebted to Shelby Foote for information about his family. For details, not all of which seem to be accurate, about Hezekiah William Foote and Huger Lee Foote, see *Biographical and Historical Memoirs of Mississippi* (Chicago: Goodspeed Publishing Co., 1891), 1:748–50.

34. Authors' interview with Shelby Foote, Memphis, 14 April 1979.

35. Carr, p. 21.

36. James E. Kibler, Jr., "Shelby Foote: A Bibliography," *Mississippi Quarterly* 24 (Fall 1971):452, lists all these.

37. James E. Kibler, Jr., "Shelby Foote," *Dictionary of Literary Biography* (Detroit: Gale, 1978), 2:148.

38. Ibid.

39. Ibid., pp. 148–49.

40. See Kibler, "Bibliography," pp. 453–55.

*Chapter Two*

1. Evans Harrington, "Interview with Shelby Foote," *Mississippi Quarterly* 24 (Fall 1971):374, 350, 373.

2. See treatment of this theme in Thomas H. Landess, "Southern History and Manhood: Major Themes in the Works of Shelby Foote," *Mississippi Quarterly* 24 (Fall 1971):321–47.

3. Shelby Foote, *Tournament* (New York: Dial Press, 1949). Page references in the text are to this edition.

4. Harrington, p. 368.

5. John Crowe Ransom, "Conrad Sits in Twilight," *Selected Poems,* 3d ed. (New York: Alfred A. Knopf, 1969), p. 118, stanza 4, lines 1, 2.

6. Landess, p. 324, states, "As suggested by the title, life for him [Hugh Bart] is a 'tournament' in which the game itself, played by the rules, is as important as the prize."

7. For aesthetic reasons Shelby Foote omits the apostrophe in contractions in his novels except when the omission would cause misreading. Further examples of this practice will not be noted with [*sic*].

8. James E. Kibler, Jr., "Shelby Foote," in *Dictionary of Literary Biography* (Detroit: Gale, 1978), 2:150.

9. Walter Sullivan, "The Continuing Renascence: Southern Fiction in the Fifties," in *South: Modern Southern Literature in Its Cultural Setting,* ed. Louis D. Rubin, Jr., and Robert D. Jacobs (Garden City, N.Y.: Doubleday & Co., Dolphin Books, 1961), p. 379.

10. Authors' interview with Shelby Foote, Memphis, Tennessee, 14 April 1979; cf. John Graham, "Talking with Shelby Foote, June 1970," ed. George Garrett, *Mississippi Quarterly* 24 (Fall 1971):406–408.

11. See, e.g., Graham, pp. 409–10.

12. Shelby Foote, *Follow Me Down,* in *Three Novels by Shelby Foote* (New York: Dial Press, 1964), p. 233. Hereafter cited as *Three Novels.* Page numbers for the constituent novels, including also *Jordan County* and *Love in a Dry Season,* each paginated separately, are given in our text. The texts of the three novels are photo-offsets of each novel's first separate printing and the page numbers therefore identical with those in the first separate printings.

13. Sullivan, p. 379.

## Chapter Three

1. Evans Harrington, "Interview with Shelby Foote," *Mississippi Quarterly* 24 (Fall 1971):373. Cf. John Carr, "It's Worth a Grown Man's Time: Shelby Foote," in *Kite-Flying and Other Irrational Acts: Conversations with Twelve Southerners,* ed. John Carr (Baton Rouge: Louisiana State University Press, 1972), p. 31.

2. James E. Kibler, Jr., "Shelby Foote: A Bibliography," *Mississippi Quarterly* 24 (Fall 1971):443–44.

3. *Virgil's Works: The Aeneid, Eclogues, Georgics,* trans. J. W. Mackail, with an Introduction by William C. McDermott, The Modern Library (New York: Random House, 1950), pp. xvi-xvii.

4. Simone Vauthier, "The Symmetrical Design: The Structural Patterns of *Love in a Dry Season,*" *Mississippi Quarterly* 24 (Fall 1971):379–403.

5. Shelby Foote, *Love in a Dry Season* in *Three Novels* (New York: Dial Press, 1964). Page references in the text are to this edition.

6. Harrington, pp. 368–69.

7. See, e.g., Vauthier, p. 379.

8. Ibid., pp. 397–99.

*Chapter Four*

1. John Carr, "It's Worth a Grown Man's Time: Shelby Foote," in *Kite-Flying and Other Irrational Acts: Conversations with Twelve Southerners,* ed. John Carr (Baton Rouge: Louisiana State University Press, 1972), p. 19.

2. Evans Harrington, "Interview with Shelby Foote," *Mississippi Quarterly* 24 (Fall 1971):357.

3. See Philippe Jaworski, "Terre Promise, Terre Conquise, Terre Vaine . . . ," *Delta* 4 (April 1977):43, n. 4.

4. Harrington, p. 373.

5. Shelby Foote, *Jordan County,* in *Three Novels* (New York: Dial Press, 1964). Page references in the text are to this edition.

6. James E. Kibler, Jr., "Shelby Foote: A Bibliography," *Mississippi Quarterly* 24 (Fall 1971):453, 454.

7. John Graham, "Talking with Shelby Foote, June 1970," ed. George Garrett, *Mississippi Quarterly* 24 (Fall 1971):412.

8. Ibid., pp. 412–13.

9. Harrington, p. 366.

10. See Kibler, "Bibliography," pp. 456–57.

11. Thomas H. Landess states that "one does not feel that the piece is devised to describe the ills of Southern society. . . . it is the central action . . . which is the true subject matter of the artist." He notes that in this story, "the only one which deals explicitly with the nature of art itself," Foote presents not only a totally committed artist but a man "whose other needs must be satisfied." See Landess, "Southern History and Manhood: Major Themes in the Works of Shelby Foote," *Mississippi Quarterly* 24 (Fall 1971):322, 323.

12. Carr, p. 19.

13. Kibler, "Bibliography," p. 453.

14. Ibid., p. 447.

15. Ibid., pp. 454–55, lists "Pillar of Fire" in *The Night before Chancellorsville And Other Civil War Stories,* ed. Shelby Foote (New York, 1957), pp. 125–58, as "a legitimate shorter version of the *Jordan County* 'Pillar of Fire.'"

16. Simone Vauthier, in "Pillar of Fire: The Civil War of Narratives," *Delta* 4 (May 1977):160–75, presents an exhaustive examination of the story in terms of its "ternary overall pattern."

17. See ibid., passim, for a detailed treatment of the symbolism of sun and fire.

18. Louis D. Rubin, Jr., ed., *The Literary South* (New York: John Wiley and Sons, 1979), pp. 671–82.

*Chapter Five*

1. Shelby Foote, *Shiloh* (New York: Dial Press, 1952; Apollo Editions, 1962). Page references in the text are to the latter edition.

*Chapter Six*

1. See the following entries in our "Selected Bibliography": Garrett; Rubin; White and Sugg; Williams.
2. Daniel Hoffman, ed., *Harvard Guide to Contemporary American Writing* (Cambridge, Mass.: Harvard University Press, Belknap Press, 1979), p. 184.
3. John Cournos, review of *The Civil War: A Narrative*, vol. 1: *Fort Sumter to Perryville*, by Shelby Foote, in *Commonweal*, 9 January 1959, p. 393.
4. C. Vann Woodward, "The Great American Butchery," review of *The Civil War: A Narrative*, vol. 3: *Red River to Appomattox*, by Shelby Foote, in *New York Review of Books*, 6 March 1975, p. 12.
5. James I. Robertson, Jr., review of *The Civil War: A Narrative*, vol. 2: *Fredericksburg to Meridian*, in *American Historical Review* 69 (April 1964):791–92.
6. Allan Nevins, James I. Robertson, Jr., Bell I. Wiley, eds., *Civil War Books: A Critical Bibliography*, 2 vols. (Baton Rouge: Louisiana State University Press, 1967–69), 2: s.v. "Catton," "Foote," "Nevins."
7. Robert Hartje, review of *The Civil War: A Narrative*, vol. 3: *Red River to Appomattox*, in *American Historical Review* 81 (October 1976):975–76.
8. James I. Robertson Jr., review of *The Civil War: A Narrative*, by Shelby Foote, in *Civil War History* 21 (June 1975):172.
9. Ibid., pp. 173, 174, 175.
10. Oscar Handlin, *Truth in History* (Cambridge, Mass.: Harvard University Press, 1979), pp. 57–58; 67.
11. Ibid., pp. 58, 60.
12. Ibid., p. 61.
13. Ibid., pp. 61, 409.
14. Morton White, *Foundations of Historical Knowledge* (New York: Harper & Row, 1965), pp. 5–6.
15. W. B. Gallie, *Philosophy and the Historical Understanding* (New York: Schocken Books, 1964), pp. 24, 31, 84.
16. Ibid., pp. 90, 91–92.
17. Leo Braudy, *Narrative Form in History and Fiction* (Princeton, N.J.: Princeton University Press, 1970), pp. 5, 7.

18. Ibid., pp. 34, 88.
19. Ibid., pp. 3, 211, 214.
20. Ibid., pp. 12–13, 239.
21. Ibid., p. 261.
22. Woodward, p. 12.
23. John Keegan, *The Face of Battle* (New York: Viking Press, 1976), pp. 54, 61.
24. Ibid., pp. 57–62.
25. Ibid., pp. 62–69.
26. Shelby Foote, "The Novelist's View of History," *Mississippi Quarterly* 17 (Fall 1964):219–20.
27. Ibid., pp. 220–21.
28. Ibid., pp. 223–24.
29. Evans Harrington, "Interview with Shelby Foote," *Mississippi Quarterly* 24 (Fall 1971):357, 358.
30. John Carr, "It's Worth a Grown Man's Time: Shelby Foote," in *Kite-Flying and Other Irrational Acts: Conversations with Twelve Southerners,* ed. John Carr (Baton Rouge: Louisiana State University Press, 1972), p. 10.
31. Ibid., p. 15.
32. John Graham, "Talking with Shelby Foote," June 1970, ed. George Garrett, *Mississippi Quarterly* 24 (Fall 1971):418–19.
33. Braudy, p. 242.
34. Shelby Foote, *The Civil War: A Narrative,* vol. 1: *Fort Sumter to Perryville*; vol. 2, *Fredericksburg to Meridian*; vol, 3: *Red River to Appomattox*; 3 vols. (New York: Random House, 1958–74). Cited by volume and page number in the text.
35. Cf. Dick Cavett, Interview with Shelby Foote, New Orleans, Winter 1979; aired on PBS in Memphis 21 February 1979.
36. Harrington, p. 353.
37. Wirt Williams, "Shelby Foote's *Civil War*: The Novelist as Humanistic Historian," *Mississippi Quarterly* 24 (Fall 1971):435–36.
38. John Crowe Ransom, "Antique Harvesters," *Selected Poems,* 3d ed. (New York: Alfred A. Knopf, 1969), p. 83.
39. Eudora Welty, "Place in Fiction," in *The Eye of the Story: Selected Essays and Reviews,* Vintage Books (New York: Random House, 1979), pp. 122, 127–28.
40. Ibid., p. 126.
41. C. Vann Woodward, *The Burden of Southern History,* rev. ed. (Baton Rouge: Louisiana State University Press, 1968), p. 21.
42. Cf. Harrington, p. 370.
43. Cf. Foote, "Novelist's View of History," pp. 221–23.

44. Ibid., p. 221.

45. Robertson, review of *The Civil War,* 3 vols., p. 174.

46. George Garrett, "Foote's *The Civil War*: The Version for Posterity?" *Mississippi Quarterly* 28 (Winter 1974–75):87–88.

47. Ibid., p. 89.


*Chapter Seven*

1. Evans Harrington, "Interview with Shelby Foote," *Mississippi Quarterly* 24 (Fall 1971):357.

2. George Garrett, "Foote's *The Civil War:* The Version for Posterity?" *Mississippi Quarterly* 28 (Winter 1974–75):86.

3. Review of *Follow Me Down,* by Shelby Foote, in *Times Literary Supplement,* 3 August 1951, p. 481.

4. Garrett, pp. 86–87.

5. Walter Sullivan, "The Continuing Renascence: Southern Fiction in the Fifties," in *South: Modern Southern Literature in Its Cultural Setting,* ed. Louis D. Rubin, Jr., and Robert D. Jacobs (Garden City, N.Y.: Doubleday & Co., Dolphin Books, 1961), pp. 378–79.

6. Garrett, p. 87.

7. Quoted, ibid., from interview for *Memphis Commercial Appeal,* 15 July 1973.

8. Shelby Foote, *September September* (New York: Random House, 1978). Page numbers in the text refer to this edition.

9. William Thomas, "Appomattox for Shelby Foote," *Memphis Commercial Appeal Mid-South Magazine,* 19 March 1978, p. 23.

10. Ibid., p. 25. Cf. *September September,* p. 80

11. Dean Flower, "The Way We Live Now," review of eight novels including *September September,* by Shelby Foote, in *Hudson Review* 31 (Summer 1978):343–55.

12. James E. Kibler, Jr., "Shelby Foote," in *Dictionary of Literary Biography* (Detroit: Gayle, 1978), 2:153.

13. Thomas, p. 25.

14. Philippe Jaworski, "Terre Promise, Terre Conquise, Terre Vaine . . .," *Delta* 4 (May 1977): 33, 34. The first quotation is as follows: "La question . . . est donc celle de la nature du discours de l'Histoire: il s'agit de savoir comment *dire* l'Histoire." The second: "C'est en effet dans cette section centrale ["Child by Fever"] que se trouve établi un rapport de vérité entre le déchiffrement de l'Histoire et un récit dont le producteur serait tout à la fois extérieur au contenu narratif et capable d'explorer le secret de ses profondeurs. C'est la formule *romanesque,* ouvertement et délibérément

romanesque, qui peut, seule, ne rien savoir et cependant tout connaître, tout
ignorer et tout dire, mentir et dire vrai."

    15. Ibid., p. 34. The French phrase is: ". . . la logique et le privilège de
l'écriture romanesque."

# Selected Bibliography

PRIMARY SOURCES

1. Collected Editions
*Three Novels. Follow Me Down, Jordan County, Love in a Dry Season.* New York: The Dial Press, 1964.

2. Fiction
*Follow Me Down.* New York: Dial Press, Inc., 1950. Reprints: New York: New American Library (Signet), 1951; New York: Random House, 1978; New York: Ballantine Books, Inc., 1981.
*Jordan County: A Landscape in Narrative.* New York: The Dial Press, 1954.
*Love in a Dry Season.* New York: The Dial Press, 1951. Reprints: New York: New American Library (Signet), 1952; New York: Random House, 1979; New York: Ballantine Books, Inc., 1981.
*The Merchant of Bristol.* Greenville, Miss.: The Levee Press, June 1947.
*September September.* New York: Random House, 1978. Reprint: New York: Ballantine Books, Inc., 1979.
*Shiloh.* New York: The Dial Press, 1952. Reprints: New York: New American Library (Signet), 1954, 1961; New York: The Dial Press (Apollo), [1962]; New York: Random House, 1976; New York: Ballantine Books, Inc., 1981.
*Tournament.* New York: Dial Press, Inc., 1949.

3. History
*The Civil War: A Narrative.* Vol. 1: *Fort Sumter to Perryville.* New York: Random House, 1958.
*The Civil War: A Narrative.* Vol. 2: *Fredericksburg to Meridian.* New York: Random House, 1963.
*The Civil War: A Narrative.* Vol. 3: *Red River to Appomattox.* New York: Random House, 1974.

4. Edited Work
*The Night Before Chancellorsville and Other Civil War Stories.* Edited by Shelby Foote. New York: New American Library (Signet), 1957.

5. Essays
"A Colloquim with Shelby Foote" (with Helen White and Redding Sugg).
*Southern Humanities Review* 15 (Fall 1981):281–299.
"Faulkner's Depiction of the Planter Aristocracy" (pp. 40–61), "Faulkner
and Race" (pp. 86–103), "Faulkner and War" (pp. 156–67). In *The
South and Faulkner's Yoknapatawpha: The Actual and the Apocryphal.*
Edited by Evans Harrington and Ann J. Abadie. Jackson: University
Press of Mississippi, 1977.
"The Novelist's View of History." *Mississippi Quarterly* 17 (Fall 1964):219–
25.
*The Novelist's View of History.* Winston-Salem, N.C.: Palaemon Press Lim-
ited, 1981.


SECONDARY SOURCES


1. Bibliographical
Kibler, James E., Jr. "Shelby Foote: A Bibliography." *Mississippi Quarterly*
24 (Fall 1971):437–65. Indispensable. Complete to date of publication. Formal description of all Foote's books; lists reprints, foreign
editions; includes pertinent information about them. Lists poetry
(juvenilia), short stories (including juvenilia), drama, nonfiction, lec-
tures, with brief comments. Brief annotation of interviews, articles;
lists a number of contemporary reviews. French scholars adapted this
bibliography and brought it up to date in *Delta* 4 (May 1977):181–89.

2. Special Issues of Periodicals
*Delta* 4 (May 1977). Special issue devoted to *Jordan County,* edited by Claude
Richard. [This review is published by the Centre d'Étude et de Re-
cherches sur les Écrivains du Sud aux États-Unis, Université Paul
Valéry, Montpellier.] Contains nine articles on different components of
*Jordan County,* with concentration on "A Marriage Portion," the most
intensive though often abstruse analysis any of Foote's books has received. Introduction useful for the insight it gives into Foote's reputation in France. The articles most accessible to American students are
listed and annotated separately below.
*Mississippi Quarterly* 24 (Fall 1971). Special issue devoted to Foote, still the
best single source on the various aspects of his work. The most significant articles are here separately listed and annotated.

3. Articles and Parts of Books
Bradford, M. E. "Else We Should Love It Too Well." *National Review,* 14

February 1975, pp. 174–75. One of the abler assessments of *The Civil War* following publication of vol. 3.

Breit, Harvey. "Talk with Shelby Foote." *New York Times Book Review,* 27 April 1952, p. 16. Influential early review-interview; discusses *Shiloh* and provides biography.

Carr, John. "'Because I Loved America.'" *Figaro* (New Orleans), 3 December 1979, sec. II, pp. 11–14. Interview in Memphis contains some remarks about Hemingway, Faulkner; Foote looks back over years of writing *The Civil War.* Biographical account contains some factual errors.

————. "It's Worth a Grown Man's Time: Shelby Foote." In *Kite-Flying and Other Irrational Acts: Conversations with Twelve Southerners,* pp. 3–33. Edited by John Carr. Baton Rouge: Louisiana State University Press, 1972. Reprinted from *Contempora* 1 (July-August 1970):2–16. Significant for Foote's comments on history, literature, and recent history of his own region.

Garrett, George. "Foote's *The Civil War:* The Version for Posterity?" *Mississippi Quarterly* 28 (Winter 1974–75):83–92. Review-essay on completed history placed in context of Foote's work to date. Examines the "Bibliographical Note" at end of each volume, the soundness of Foote's scholarship, and his attitudes. Discusses literary techniques applied to the writing of the history; centers on characterization. Concludes that ". . . the work is, without question or qualification, a masterpiece, one of the very few genuinely great literary works of our time. Time will tell."

Graham, John. "Talking with Shelby Foote, June 1970." Edited by George Garrett. *Mississippi Quarterly* 24 (Fall 1971):405–27. Transcribed from four tapes for broadcasts of "The Scholar's Bookshelf," a fifteen-minute radio program conducted by Professor John Graham of the University of Virginia. [Taped June 19, 1970, Hollins College.] Centers first on structure and method of *Follow Me Down*; second, on "Ride Out" and jazz; third, on the writing of history and related matters; fourth, on Foote's reading.

Harrington, Evans. "Interview with Shelby Foote." *Mississippi Quarterly* 24 (Fall 1971):349–77. Interview in Foote's home in Memphis, June 1968. Himself a novelist and able scholar and critic, Harrington conducted a well-structured, highly informative interview on a wide range of subjects: beginning of Foote's career; his reading and opinions of authors; ideas and attitudes that govern Foote's writing.

Hartje, Robert. Review of *The Civil War: A Narrative.* Vol. 3: *Red River to Appomattox. American Historical Review* 81 (October 1976):975–76. Significant as evidence of increasing approval among professional historians of Foote's work in their field. Should be compared with review of vol. 2 in same journal, by Robertson, listed below.

Howell, Elmo. "The Greenville Writers and the Mississippi Country People." *Louisiana Studies* 8 (Winter 1969):348–60. Discusses Hodding Carter, David L. Cohn, Foote, William Alexander Percy in context of differences between Mississippi hill people and Deltans. Judges Foote's Jordan County materials from the hillman's point of view.

Jaworski, Philippe. "Terre Promise, Terre Conquise, Terre Vaine . . ." ["Promised Land, Conquered Land, Waste Land . . ."]. *Delta* 4 (May 1977):25–43. Summary statement of the "thematic and ideological content" ("contenu thématique-idéologique") of *Jordan County* as a whole followed by analysis of its "two structures," the linear and the geometric. Graphically illustrates "the triangular figure that shapes the book" ("la figure triangulaire que dessine le livre"). Subtly discusses interrelationships of the seven component stories and the two structures within which they are set to make interesting case for the artistic unity of the book.

Kibler, James E., Jr. "Shelby Foote." In *Dictionary of Literary Biography*, 2:148–54. Detroit: Gale, 1978. Succinct biography. Discussion of works in chronological order, with particular attention to *September September;* work in progress; reputation. Short bibliography.

Landess, Thomas H. "Southern History and Manhood: Major Themes in the Works of Shelby Foote." *Mississippi Quarterly* 24 (Fall 1971):321–47. Most valuable article on Foote to date of publication. Thematic study of novels, first two volumes of the history. Points out interrelationships among stories, novels, the history and credits Foote with creation of his own "antimyth" in opposition to "rigid and persuasive" Southern mythology. Misreads *The Civil War* in regard to Foote's view of "political implications" and Lincoln's character and career, but highly appreciative of other aspects.

Robertson, James I., Jr. Review of *The Civil War: A Narrative*. Vol. 2: *Fredericksburg to Meridian*. *American Historical Review* 69 (April 1964):790–91.

———. Review of *The Civil War: A Narrative*. 3 vols. *Civil War History* 21 (June 1975):172–75. These reviews should be read with that of Hartje, above, as evidence of the changing attitudes of academic historians toward Foote's *Civil War*.

Rubin, Louis, D., Jr. "Shelby Foote's Civil War." *Prospects: An Annual Journal of American Studies* 1 (1974):313–33. Assesses Foote's completed history against background of acquaintance with the author and the outpouring of Civil War books preceding and during celebration of the Centennial. Discusses treatment of Lee and Longstreet, Lincoln, Grant; compares it with that by other writers such as Douglas Southall Freeman. Emphasizes Foote's freedom from partisanship, stresses literary quality of the work, which he judges "the classic full-length presentation of the American Civil War, worthy to stand alongside the great works of narrative history."

Sullivan, Walter. "The Continuing Renascence: Southern Fiction in the Fifties." In *South: Modern Southern Literature in Its Cultural Setting,* pp. 376–91. Edited by Louis D. Rubin, Jr., and Robert D. Jacobs. Garden City, N.Y.: Doubleday & Co., Dolphin Books, 1961. Southern novelist, critic, and teacher discusses Foote first among "an even dozen" writers who have emerged since World War II. Chooses *Follow Me Down* to illustrate Foote's moral concerns; points out differences from William Faulkner.

Thomas, William. "Appomattox for Shelby Foote." *Memphis Commercial Appeal Mid-South Magazine,* 19 March 1978, pp. 22–25. Reports visit to Foote in his home; quotes him on *September September,* literary influences, retrospective remarks on *Civil War*; brief comment on "Two Gates to the City."

Vauthier, Simone. "The Symmetrical Design: The Structural Patterns of *Love in a Dry Season." Mississippi Quarterly* 24 (Fall 1971):379–403. Detailed analysis by French scholar (University of Strasbourg). Explicates "intricate" structural pattern, involving "two basic narrative structures, dual or ternary," of the novel. Analyzes voyeur theme in terms of characters "seeing" and "being seen"; reversals of function; symbolism; and "repetitions and variations of verbal patterns."

―――. "'Pillar of Fire': The Civil War of Narratives." *Delta* 4 (May 1977):159–75. Examination of structure, Lundy's first-person, two-part narrative enclosing tripartite "meta-story" of Isaac Jameson's life by omniscient narrator. Argues that "the story exists only in the torsion of its two strands and their unresolved tension," stresses the "intertextuality" of the story, and infers Foote's purpose is "to make us aware that truth whether of history or fiction is a construction."

White, Helen, and Sugg, Redding S., Jr. "Shelby Foote's *Iliad." Virginia Quarterly Review* 55 (Spring 1979):234–50. Descriptive account of *The Civil War* stressing its quality as history at the level of literature, the *Iliad* being a model and touchstone. Attention to status of narrative and military history; Foote's scholarship, modernism, Southern qualities; tone, style, organization, and characterization.

Williams, Wirt. "Shelby Foote's *Civil War*: The Novelist as Humanistic Historian." *Mississippi Quarterly* 24 (Fall 1971):429–36. Examines first two volumes as literature, "humanistic history," and traces parallels between Foote's narrative history and fiction and drama.

Woodward, C. Vann. "The Great American Butchery." Review of *The Civil War: A Narrative.* Vol. 3: *Red River to Appomattox. New York Review of Books,* 6 March 1975, p. 12. Discusses *The Civil War* in light of professional historians' attitudes toward narrative and particularly military history. Somewhat guardedly states Foote's focus on "guns-and-battle aspect of war" is right for his "impressive narrative gifts and . . . dramatic purposes." Also warns "psychohistorians," "cliometricians," and "crypto-analysts" that Foote's work may "expose them to the terrifying chaos and mystery of their intractable subject and disabuse them of some of their illusions of mastery."

# Index

74, 79, cross-references in, 79, 80–82; points of view, 70–71; unifying tone, source of, 71–74, 79

*Tournament,* 15, 16, 17, 20, 25, 26, 28, 39, 41, 42, 43, 49, 61, 62, 64, 124, 126, 127; canon, position in, 21; composition of, 16; musical aspects, 22–23; protagonist modeled on H. L. Foote, 22; structure of, 23–25; themes of, 20–22; title, significance of, 23

Work in progress, 131–32

WORKS: HISTORY

The Civil War. Vol. 1: *Fort Sumter to Perryville.* Vol. 2: *Fredericksburg to Meridian.* Vol. 3: *Red River to Appomattox,* 1, 18, 26, 30, 82–83, 126, 128, 132; characterization in, 115–23, examples of, 118–22; critics' response to, 84–87; epic design of, 111–13; humor in, 104–107; the *Iliad* and, 100, 111–13, 126; modernism in, 100–102; narrative voice in, 96, 97, 107–10; novels among sources of, 99; place, rendering of, 102–104; plotting of, 110–15; sources and methods, 96–100; Southern qualities, 102–107; themes, structural use of, 113–15; tragic elements, 107

Foote, Shelby Dade Sr., 14, 15

*Go Down, Moses* (Faulkner), 49

*God Shakes Creation* (Cohn), 8. *See Where I Was Born and Raised.*

*Great Gatsby, The,* (Fitzgerald), 46

Greenville, Miss., model for Bristol, 1; literary atmosphere, 9–10

Hill country (of Miss.), physical and cultural peculiarities of, 2, 5

Hoffman, Malvina, 7

Jordan County, compared with Yoknapatawpha, 19–20; conceived as "landscape in narrative," 19–20, 49; modeled on Washington Co., Miss., 1; work in progress on, 131–32

Joyce, James, 17

*Lanterns on the Levee* (Percy), on the Delta, physical features of, 6–7, social classes in, 7–8; influence on SF, 6

*Light in August* (Faulkner), 15

Military history, status of, 85, 92–93

Mounds Plantation, 13, 14

Mt. Holly Plantation, 7, 13; model for Solitaire, 14, 62

Narrative history, validity of, 87–92

Nevins, Allan, 85, 86

North Carolina, Univ. of, 16

Percy, Walker, 6, 10, 16, 17

Percy, William Alexander, 6–8, 9, 12, 15, 17

Percy, LeRoy, 7–8, 12, 23

Peters, Minnie, 14